The Theological Imagination

How can we live truthfully in a world riddled with ambiguity, contradiction, and clashing viewpoints? We make sense of the world imaginatively, resolving ambiguous and incomplete impressions into distinct forms and wholes. But the images, objects, words, and even lives of which we make sense in this way always have more or other possible meanings. Judith Wolfe argues that faith gives us courage both creatively to shape our world and reverently to let things be more than we can imagine. Drawing on complementary materials from literature, psychology, art, and philosophy, her remarkable book demonstrates that Christian theology offers a potent way of imagining the world even as it brings us to the limits of our capacity to imagine. In revealing the significance of unseen depths – of what does not yet make sense to us, and of what is still incomplete – Wolfe characterizes faith as trust in God that surpasses all imagination.

JUDITH WOLFE is Professor of Philosophical Theology at the University of St Andrews. She was educated in Vienna, Jerusalem, and Oxford, and has previously taught in Oxford and Berlin. She writes, edits, and leads collaborative work in philosophical theology and in theology and the arts. Her previous publications include *Heidegger's Eschatology* (Oxford University Press, 2013) *Heidegger and Theology* (T&T Clark, 2014), and *The Oxford Handbook of Nineteenth-Century Christian Thought* (Oxford University Press, 2017, co-edited with Joel D. S. Rasmussen and Johannes Zachhuber). In 2022 she delivered the historic Hulsean Lectures (upon which this book is based) at the University of Cambridge.

CURRENT ISSUES IN THEOLOGY

General Editors:
Iain Torrance
Pro-Chancellor of the University of Aberdeen

David Fergusson
University of Edinburgh

Editorial Advisory Board:
David Ford   *University of Cambridge*
Bryan Spinks   *Yale University*
Kathryn Tanner   *Yale Divinity School*

There is a need among upper-undergraduate and graduate students of theology, as well as among Christian teachers and church professionals, for a series of short, focussed studies of particular key topics in theology written by prominent theologians. Current Issues in Theology meets this need.

The books in the series are designed to provide a 'state-of-the-art' statement on the topic in question, engaging with contemporary thinking as well as providing original insights. The aim is to publish books which stand between the static monograph genre and the more immediate statement of a journal article, by authors who are questioning existing paradigms or rethinking perspectives.

Other titles in the series:

Holy Scripture   John Webster
The Just War Revisited   Oliver O'Donovan
Bodies and Souls, or Spirited Bodies?   Nancey Murphy
Christ and Horrors   Marilyn McCord Adams
Divinity and Humanity   Oliver D. Crisp
The Eucharist and Ecumenism   George Hunsinger
Christ the Key   Kathryn Tanner
Theology without Metaphysics   Kevin W. Hector
Reconsidering John Calvin   Randall C. Zachman
God's Presence   Frances Youngman

JUDITH WOLFE
University of St Andrews

The Theological Imagination
Perception and Interpretation in Life, Art, and Faith

CAMBRIDGE
UNIVERSITY PRESS

Shaftesbury Road, Cambridge CB2 8EA, United Kingdom

One Liberty Plaza, 20th Floor, New York, NY 10006, USA

477 Williamstown Road, Port Melbourne, VIC 3207, Australia

314–321, 3rd Floor, Plot 3, Splendor Forum, Jasola District Centre,
New Delhi – 110025, India

103 Penang Road, #05–06/07, Visioncrest Commercial, Singapore 238467

Cambridge University Press is part of Cambridge University Press & Assessment,
a department of the University of Cambridge.

We share the University's mission to contribute to society through the pursuit of
education, learning and research at the highest international levels of excellence.

www.cambridge.org
Information on this title: www.cambridge.org/9781009519861

DOI: 10.1017/9781009519847

First published 2024

Printed in the United Kingdom by TJ Books Limited, Padstow Cornwall

A catalogue record for this publication is available from the British Library

*A Cataloging-in-Publication data record for this book is available from the
Library of Congress*

ISBN 978-1-009-51986-1 Hardback

Contents

Figures

Acknowledgements

The substance of this book was presented as the Hulsean Lectures 2022 at the University of Cambridge. I am grateful to the Electors and hosts, especially the Regius Professor David Fergusson, for their hospitality; and to all who attended and engaged with them, especially Douglas Hedley, Janet and Oliver Soskice, and Andrew Wilson. While delivered in Cambridge, the lectures were conceived at the School of Divinity of the University of St Andrews and its Institute for Theology, Imagination and the Arts. I owe much to my local colleagues and students, who accompanied this work from the beginning and discussed it in various forums, including a series of seminars on the Hulsean Lectures. Special thanks to Brendan Wolfe; to respondents Euan Grant, Trevor Hart, Gavin Hopps, Oliver O'Donovan, George Pattison, and Andrew Torrance; to my PhD students, especially Patrick McGlinchey and Charles Howell; and to Christoph Schwöbel, whose lasting influence continues to shape our work together. Beyond St Andrews, friends and colleagues have enriched this book with their critical engagement and their own theological imagination; I am enduringly grateful to them, especially Sean Dimond, Chris Insole, Karen Kilby, Jean-Luc Marion, John Milbank, Stephen Mulhall, Simon Oliver, Thomas Pfau, Catherine Pickstock, Brian

Robinette, and Eleonore Stump. Beyond all universities, this book could not have been conceived without my family, who inspired and accompanied it: To Marina, Bill, Fritzi, Brendan, Tobias, Nathaniel, and Miriam, as well as other kin near and far, I am grateful for countless gifts.

I am grateful also to those who invited me to give other lectures and seminars that nurtured the growth of this book, and to those that attended them: at the Colloque Castelli, the American Philosophical Association (Central Division), the British Society for the Philosophy of Religion, the Image as Theology project, the Religion & Literature Group at the University of Notre Dame, Pusey House Oxford, the D Society at the University of Cambridge, the Theology Seminar at King's College London, the Theology & Ethics Seminar at Durham University, the Centre for Protestant Thought at the University of Aberdeen, the Philosophy & Theology Reading Group, and my St Andrews Doktorantenkreis.

Research underpinning especially Chapters 1 and 3, as well as the reproduction of images in this book, were generously funded by Templeton Religion Trust grants *Mapping the Imagination* (TRT0354) and *Art as Revelation* (TRT0391). I am indebted to the Trust staff, the project team, and especially to discussions with my research associate, psychologist of art Dr Marina Iosifyan.

Versions of some of the material in this book have appeared in other publications: the journals *Religion & Literature*, *Modern Theology*, and the *European Journal of Philosophy of Religion*, as well as the collection *Image as Theology*, edited by Casey Strine, Mark McInroy, and Alexis

Torrance, and the *T&T Clark Companion to Theology and the Arts*, edited by Stephen Garrett and Imogen Adkins. Materials are re-used here with kind permission of the editors.

Copyright information for all images is detailed in the captions. Permission for extracts from poems by T. S. Eliot was kindly granted by Faber (UK & international) and HarperCollins (USA). Epigraph translations are mine. Biblical texts are quoted according to the anglicized *New Revised Standard Version*, except where otherwise indicated. The team at Cambridge University Press has been exemplary, and I thank especially Beatrice Rehl, Liz Davey, and Swati Kumari for their expert and patient collaboration. For negotiating permissions, preparing the back matter, and for her patience, advice, and friendship throughout the process I am deeply grateful to Dr Margaret McKerron.

1 | Introduction

Imagining a World

And the attentive animals are already aware
that we are not quite reliably at home
in the interpreted world.
R. M. Rilke (1875–1926), 'First Duino Elegy'

Finding and Making

This book is about how to imagine the world theologically.
By this I do not intend to say that theological thought is
imaginative, let alone imaginary, more markedly than any
other kind of thought. Rather, I take *all* our orientation in
the world to be, to some extent, imaginative. 'Imagination',
as I use the term, is not primarily the capacity to picture
absent or fictional things. Rather, it is first and foremost the
power to make the continuous stream of sense perception
meaningful by integrating discrete data points into forms
or wholes (what the Germans would call *Gestalt*).[1] In Mary
Warnock's classic summary of this definition, drawing on
the tradition of Hume, Kant, and many others,

> we use imagination in our ordinary perception of the world.
> This perception cannot be separated from interpretation.
> Interpretation can be common to everyone, and in this sense

ordinary, or it can be inventive, personal and revolutionary. So imagination is necessary … to enable us to recognise things in the world as familiar, to take for granted features of the world which we need to take for granted and rely on, if we are to go about our ordinary business; but it is also necessary if we are to see the world as significant of something unfamiliar, if we are ever to treat the objects of perception as symbolising or suggesting things other than themselves.[2]

To put it differently, ordinary seeing – the ability to organize the sensory field into discrete objects – involves imaginative *acts*, which are no less active for remaining unnoticed. Seeing involves the assimilation of data points to perceptual patterns that we have inherited or acquired, and which we continue to update in response to ongoing experience. These integrative processes are not, for the most part, subject to conscious inspection: they form part of the very act of seeing and understanding, and so usually occur unconsciously. Both Hume and Kant were enduringly bewildered by them. Hume marvels that 'ideas are thus collected by a kind of magical faculty of the soul, which … is inexplicable by the utmost efforts of human understanding'.[3] And Kant describes the imagination as a kind of wizard behind a curtain, 'a hidden art in the depths of the human soul, whose real modes of activity nature is hardly likely ever to allow us to discover, and to have open to our gaze'.[4]

What is true of ordinary perception is intensified in the perception of created images, of pictures. The ability to see these strokes as a cube (Fig. 1), these blotches as lilies (Fig. 2), or these lines as a smile (Fig. 3) involves active projection and completion, by matching lines and colours whose

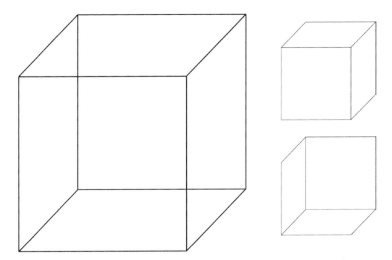

Fig. 1 *Necker's Cube*, 2006. Digital illustration.

Fig. 2 Claude Monet, *Water Lilies in Giverny*, 1917. Oil on canvas, 100.3 × 200.5 cm; Musée d'Arts de Nantes, Nantes, France.

meaning is not fully determined by their two-dimensional appearance to memories of spatial and psychological depth, and thus completing the appearance in front of us. These acts of seeing are not guaranteed by either the images

Fig. 3 Leonardo da Vinci, *Mona Lisa*, c. 1503–1506. Oil on poplar panel, 77.0 × 53.2 cm; Louvre, Paris, France.

or our memories and patterns: they are co-creative and exceed the calculus of correspondence.

But images are not the only objects which we *see* only by perceiving in them a depth that is not fully contained in their lines and colours. It is not only the mystery of the *Mona Lisa*, but also the mood and character of the people around us that we grasp imaginatively by attending to their faces. Like Mona Lisa's, a baby's smile (Fig. 4) is at once a matter of immediate seeing and one of imaginative projection. Of course, there is often a truth of the matter – but not always. Like our appreciation of artworks, our perception of faces can never fully evade the risk of mis- or overinterpretation; on the contrary, such vulnerability to deception is integral to what it means to see a face at all.[5] This ambiguity

Fig. 4 Ruizluquepaz, *Portrait of a One-Year-Old Boy at Sunset*, undated. Photograph; Buenos Aires, Argentina. Credit: Ruizluquepaz / E+ via Getty Images.

Fig. 5 Matt Anderson Photography, *Valley of Fire Hillside Ghosts*, undated. Photograph. Credit: Matt Anderson Photography / Moment Collection via Getty Images.

is refracted in our ability to appreciate actors on stage or see expressive faces even where there are none (Fig. 5).

And if we cannot see images or faces without imaginatively projecting the spatial and psychological depth that makes sense of them, then the same is true in more subtle and intricate ways of our ability imaginatively to grasp actions and

Fig. 6 Rogistok, *Push the Red Button*, undated. Digital illustration. Credit: Adobe Stock.

even entire lives. To see in a finger movement a crime against humanity (Fig. 6), and in a step forward an act of bravery (Fig. 7), requires imaginative projection, informed by memories, expectations, myths, values, and fears. We do not overlay these meanings as belated, optional interpretations on a more basic, neutral perception of component elements: rather, we take in an action and divine its meaning in a single movement. This means that our way of seeing the world is at once immediate and mediating, not merely a matter of finding but always also one of making. This holds both danger and promise. On the one hand, as Pascal observed in his critique of the imagination, it lifts experience from the safe ground of reason: 'The imagination holds sway over everything. It creates beauty, justice, and happiness, which is the entirety of the world.'[6] On the other, as the Romantics realized, it makes us capable of

Fig. 7 Conrad Schmitt Studios, *Martyrdom of St Maximillian Kolbe*, 2014. Stained glass window; Pope St. John Paul II Chapel, University of the Lake, Mundelein, IL. Credit: Original design and creation by Conrad Schmitt Studios. Photo: Fr. Gaurav Schroff.

being co-creators with God. In Coleridge's famous line, 'The primary imagination I hold to be the living Power and prime Agent of all human Perception, and as a repetition in the finite mind of the eternal act of creation in the infinite I Am.'[7]

You will notice the analogical structure of this concept of imagination. It claims that analogous things go on in our perception of everyday objects and images (as in Figs. 1 and 2), our perception of persons and their actions (as in Figs. 4, 6, and 7), our understanding of our own and others' lives, and our way of seeing the world as a whole, our worldview. These include habitual misperceptions (as in Fig. 5) and perceptions to which the terms 'correct' and 'incorrect' cannot easily be applied. On each of these levels, there is a constant interplay of finding and making: a confrontation with disparate data points which our minds integrate into wholes – into objects, persons, and narratives, and into a whole world with depth and continuity.

In saying this, I am not advancing a radically constructivist view of perception, but rather, to use art historian Ernst Gombrich's term, talking about 'the beholder's share'.[8] In other words, I am taking a broadly phenomenological approach, investigating how phenomena are constituted for us. As Merleau-Ponty puts it: 'Phenomenology … is as painstaking as the works of Balzac, Proust, Valéry or Cézanne – by reason of the same kind of attentiveness and wonder, the same demand for awareness, the same will to seize the meaning of the world or of history as that meaning comes into being.'[9]

Neither is it the primary objective of my account to construct a *model* of the imagination, much less to defend an ontological account of a human faculty called 'imagination' distinct from reason, faith, will, or other putative faculties. If I sometimes reify the imagination, it is only heuristically, not in the sense of a faculty psychology. Many philosophers and psychologists have developed related accounts of human perception using different terms: Wertheimer's 'Gestalt theory', Wittgenstein's idea of 'seeing-as', Merleau-Ponty's phenomenologically dense concept of 'perception'.[10] By using the term 'imagination', I am not constructing a model but bringing a pattern into view (which of course means that I am, in my own terms, doing imaginative work).

The risk remains that I am speaking at a level of generalization or abstraction which, from a psychological point of view, seems nonsensical. Contemporary psychology typically approaches perception and cognition functionally rather than ontologically: it describes perceptual and cognitive processes that involve a range of bodily systems, identifying the environments and factors that activate such types of processing, their variations and interrelations, and their typical failure modes.[11] Such functional approaches challenge the tendency of philosophers and theologians to ontologize human powers or faculties. At the same time, philosophical concepts such as 'imagination' can serve as focusing lenses, bundling certain processes and phenomena without necessarily adjudicating their ontological status, and can thus direct psychologists towards new questions and investigations.[12] Conversely, some psychological theories strengthen philosophical conjectures. As I have argued elsewhere, the theory of predictive processing (or predictive coding) concretizes some of my phenomenological observations by describing perception as a constant negotiation between 'bottom-up' input and 'top-down' priors, which is operative at all levels of engagement with the world.[13] It is not decisive for the arguments of this book whether we describe the imagination as a faculty, a power or a pattern of processing, or (ultimately) whether we use the term 'imagination' at all. What is decisive are observable patterns of what Heidegger calls our being-in-the-world: the ever-dynamic interplay, at all levels of this being-in-the-world, of discovery and construction.

Hiddenness and Malleability

This book starts from the intuition that our distinctive interplay of finding and making cannot be reduced to either pole: that we live neither in the naïvely realist universe of

many theologians nor in the anti-realist one of po
ernists. Rather, finding and making are inseparable,
this inseparability means that there are real stakes, real
risks, and no easy solutions. The ambiguities of invention
in its double sense of discovery and creation pervade our
self-understanding, our understanding of other people,
and our 'metaphysical dreams', including our faith.[14] Faith,
indeed, it turns out, plays a pivotal role in our understanding of imagination because it is both a species of imaginative
integration and a challenge to our need and capacity for it.

Before embarking on specific studies, I want to highlight
and discuss two aspects of the human imagination that are
central to its existential and intellectual challenge. The first
is that the activity of our imaginative integration of data into
patterns or wholes is for the most part hidden from ourselves.
It forms part of the processes of perception and understanding, and can therefore be inspected at best indirectly. In Kant's
memorable phrase, the imagination is 'a blind but indispensable function of the soul, without which we would have no
cognition at all, but of which we are seldom even conscious'.[15]

This hiddenness tends to create the illusion that there is no
creative process at all: that what we perceive is straightforwardly *found*. Hume was deeply troubled by this systematic
self-concealment. By operating habitually, he thought, the
imagination was (in Warnock's succinct paraphrase) 'not
only [a] helpful assistant [but a] deceiver, who gives us an
altogether unwarranted sense of security …. It is like a drug
without which we could not bear to inhabit the world.'[16]

It is a strong claim but one grounded in experience that we
cannot ordinarily function without such self-concealment.

When we come face to face with our own imaginative participation in the construal of things, it can propel a crisis of trust in the world: a small crisis if a leaf we picked up turned out in fact to be a bug (the inverse of Fig. 17, Chapter 3); a more profound one if we no longer trust our ability to 'read' the behaviour of those around us, as Shakespeare's Othello and Leontes find to their great cost; or worse, if we realize we might have imagined our very worldview. We usually manage these crises by immediately re-inscribing the *contrast* between fact and fiction: 'I was deluded, and the actual fact of the matter is different.' Doing so, we immediately mask our own imaginative work again.

But we need, instead, to come to terms with our irreducibly constructive, imaginative participation in the world. This is not the same as to argue, with Lyotard, Foucault, Deleuze, Butler and others, for the endless plasticity of reality within a free play of pleasure or desire.[17] Nor is it to say, with Yuval Harari and others, that our past flourishing as humans has been a function of our ability to imagine realities bigger than ourselves – gods, nations, money – which have allowed us to cooperate, but that we must now emancipate ourselves from a belief in our own imaginings and turn what used to be metaphysical *beliefs* into technical *projects*.[18] My argument is different: I affirm that we cannot neatly separate out finding from making, seeing from construing, perceiving from interpreting. But I deny that the solution is to attempt either a reduction to certainty or an emancipation into sheer construction. Our task, rather, is to learn to live in their stress field and shoulder the work of the imagination: to recognize its limits and expand its possibilities. This task is both a perpetual and a theological one, and this book is intended above all as a series of 'formal indications' (as Heidegger would call them): as ways of helping us undertake that work.[19]

The second notable aspect is the multiplicity of ways in which our imagination is conditioned. To construe objects imaginatively is to match sense impressions or other data to existing mental patterns. Philosophers from Locke and Descartes to Hume, Kant, Husserl, and Sartre, as well as psychologists of various schools, have debated the extent to which these patterns or schemata are innate or acquired and the extent to which, therefore, they are fixed or malleable. The most convincing approach, I think, is a Bayesian one in which the expectations we bring to our perceptions range from the very engrained and normative to the very flexible and ad hoc.[20] How habitually and confidently we match a set of sense impressions or data points to a mental pattern depends on how sure we are of the stability and relevance of that pattern. When we see a piece of abstract art (e.g. Fig. 8), we might be ready to believe it to depict anything or nothing, because we have no stable expectations of what sort of things an abstract painting might depict. (That said, most of us have fairly engrained opinions about the value of modern art, and thus whether or not we think there is anything to which to pay attention here in the first place.[21]) By contrast, when we see a room laid out in tiles, it is nearly impossible for us to see the room as anything *but* rectangular and the tiles as anything *but* regular because our expectations about rooms are so fixed. The Ames Room (Fig. 9) powerfully shows this force of expectation, which persists even when it forces us to see the figures as growing and shrinking.[22]

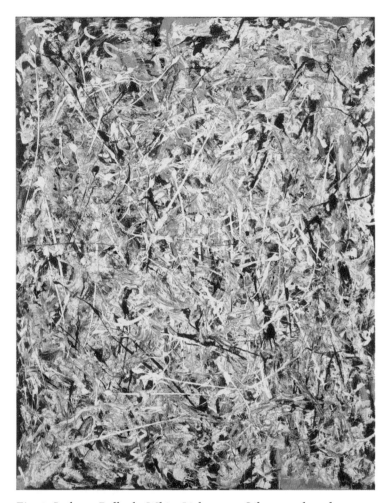

Fig. 8 Jackson Pollock, *White Light*, 1954. Oil, enamel, and aluminium paint on canvas, 122.4 × 96.9 cm; Museum of Modern Art (MoMA), New York, USA. Credit: © The Pollock-Krasner Foundation ARS, NY and DACS, London 2023. Photo: © Fine Art Images / Bridgeman Images.

Fig. 9 Maksim Popov, *Alice Is Looking for a Black Cat in a Warped Room*, 2023. Photograph; *In the Language of Rules and Exceptions: Science and Art 2023*, exhibition, Moscow Jewish Museum and Tolerance Center, Moscow, Russia. CC BY 4.0 Deed, https://commons.wikimedia.org/wiki/File:Alice_is_looking_ for_a_black_cat_in_a_warped_room.jpg.

The relevant point is that most of our imaginative work is hidden from us because most of it is not original but inherited. The patterns to which we match things are not, for the most part, ones that we individually create. Rather, our imaginations are shaped by our families, communities, and societies, whether through long-term exposure to consistent patterns or through acute and persistent reinforcement, for example by social media, political propaganda, or advertisements. Some of our convictions about the shape of things great and small, therefore, are fairly fixed, especially those that are physically grounded or deeply culturally embedded (such as the shape of rooms). Others, however, are extremely fluid; and part of what our imagination hides from itself is precisely its own malleability. We ensconce ourselves in echo chambers partly in order to constantly reinforce the hidden work of the imagination that is required to uphold a certain way of seeing the world. Once we step out of them, this way of seeing – the patterns into which we have arranged the world – may suddenly seem much less plausible. Stop watching your particular news outlet and the political scene may shift. Stop being at university and your cultural sensibilities may change. Stop going to church and the world may start to seem devoid of God.

This malleability of the imagination – of the habitual ways in which we arrange objects, people, events, and the world

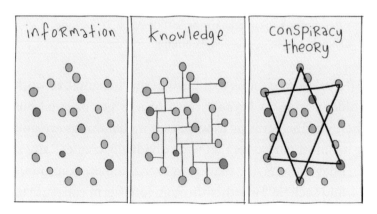

Fig. 10 Gapingvoid Culture Design Group, *Information, Knowledge, & Conspiracy Theories*, 2023. Digital illustration. Credit: Original artwork by @gapingvoid. © Image Copyright – Licensed by Gapingvoid Ltd.

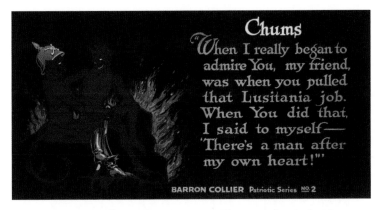

Fig. 11 Barron Collier, *Chums*, c. 1918. Photomechanical print, 27.9 × 53.3 cm; Museum of Fine Arts Boston, Boston, United States of America.

into patterns – does not itself make these arrangements arbitrary or deniable. It is an inalienable feature of our way of being in the world; there is no anti-sceptical cure that will guarantee accurate perception because that is not how perception works. However, the *malleability* of our sense of the world, on the one hand, and its habituated, largely unconscious operation – its *hiddenness* – on the other, do mean that there is a real precariousness to our ways of inhabiting the world and orienting ourselves within it. 'Knowledge' can never *conclusively* be insulated from 'conspiracy theory' (Fig. 10). And this risk is endlessly exploited by economic and political players, whose advertisements and propaganda are, above all, exercises in moulding our ways of imagining the world: associating a car with freedom (or worse, freedom with a car) or a particular political party with evil (Fig. 11). In all these cases, our associations might be as strong as they are arbitrary (Fig. 12).

*"There can be no peace until they renounce their
Rabbit God and accept our Duck God."*

Fig. 12 Paul Noth, *An Army Lines Up for Battle*, 2014. Cartoon;
New Yorker. Credit: © Paul Noth / The New Yorker Collection /
The Cartoon Bank.

What motivates this book is the dual fact that imagination is both constitutive of life in the world and irreducibly risky. We cannot but construct what we see, and this
construction is always fraught with the danger of error,
overreach, avoidance, delusion. Stanley Cavell says that

'the dangers of fraudulence, and of trust, are essential to the experience of art'.[23] They are also essential to the experience of life.

Art and Faith

The habituated process of imagining is disrupted in experiences with art. As Chapters 2, 3, and 5 will argue, works of art, literature, and music enable us to become aware of our imaginative work, and thereby expand its possibilities, loosening its rigid and restrictive habits. In this capacity, experiences with art are akin to religious experiences. Theology and religion are often seen as paradigm cases of imposing illusory patterns on the world and on people: of people pretending to find truths where they are merely imagining things, and of insisting that all phenomena fit into these supposed truths, whether or not this does violence to them. I think the opposite is true.

As Chapter 4 will argue, Christian faith is, among other things, a mode of seeing the world which beholds in that world an unseen depth of goodness, significance, and love which we do not make but in which we can participate. For the Christian faith, in other words, the human imagination is in important ways adequate to the nature of reality because our world is poetic, both in the sense that it is God's work or craft and in the sense that we do not merely apprehend but also make the world.[24]

At the same time, Christian faith also suggests that the human imagination always remains *inadequate* to God and the world: God exceeds our imagining, and the world, other people, and we ourselves have depths and complexities that remain hidden in God. To believe in God demands a commitment to not reducing the complexity of the data points before us, even at the cost of not being able to fully make sense of the world. Such commitment rests on trust that beyond any order we can impose on the world imaginatively, it is and will be held together by God. Chapters 4 and 5 will explore this dialectic of cataphasis and apophasis more fully and illuminate ways in which art, literature, and music can help sustain it.

Interdisciplinarity and Theology

The book proceeds by examining the ways we both discover and constitute the world in individual and communal life, in relation to language and vision, and in our life with art and with faith. The chapters of this book are interrelated, such that what remains unexplained or parenthetical in one is sometimes foregrounded and analyzed in another, and the arguments of all five are mutually informative. All five are also cross-disciplinary, keeping theology, philosophy, history, psychology, art history, and literary criticism in continuous conversation. Their intention is not to master these fields but to get into focus shared concerns and anxieties, confront challenges they pose to each other, unearth resources they lend each other, and formulate questions that can arise only through their dialogue. A certain lightness of tone is necessary to sustain such a conversation, and the book is mostly written in the tone – or the many tones – of the spoken voice. The text sometimes conducts quiet syntheses or takes unannounced positions within contested fields. Those interested in particular or discipline-specific discussions can find references to relevant debates and texts in the endnotes.

Despite its interdisciplinarity, the conversation staged here is at heart a theological one and is intended, among other things, to model a form of theology, one that is driven by a particular understanding of the Thomist definition of theology as the study of God and of all things in relation to God.[25] Theology, on this definition, seeks to understand a shared whole; and to do so means both to abide by its own principles and to pursue open, critical, and constructive conversations with those from other disciplines and backgrounds. Because theology relates people and fields to each other, it must be responsive to their questions, discoveries, and challenges. Being true to these challenges without thereby giving up the unique vantage point, truth claims, and intellectual and spiritual resources of theology is one of the responsibilities of contemporary theologians.

This responsibility may be realized in a variety of ways, and this book exemplifies only one of them. I want to make explicit some of the guiding intuitions of my approach, so that the arguments of this book do not appear as more, or less, or different than they are. Whether academic arguments convince us, after all, depends not only on their cogency. Rather, their cogency depends on what strikes us as plausible in the first place: what kinds of arguments can be made to count for us. And that in turn depends on our deepest intuitions of life and faith: on what trade-offs we can accept, on what we can bear, on where we think meaning should be discoverable, and on what should count as meaningless noise.[26]

Precisely because this is so, my own approach is shaped mainly by the questions arising between a Platonically inflected Thomism on the one hand and phenomenology and hermeneutics on the other. On the one hand, my approach is grounded in an ontology with realist depth, which enables certain modes of enquiry: I believe that in God all things hold together, and can therefore be investigated with courage and tenacity; that humans and all created things have dignity, and can therefore be approached with humility and empathy; and that creation is not yet finished, and can therefore be engaged with openness and creativity. On the other hand, the nature of this enquiry, in my case, is not primarily metaphysical, doctrinal, or textual. The questions asked in this book about the imagination do not begin with a metaphysical account of the world ('What metaphysical structures underlie this experience?'), with a doctrine ('What is the trinitarian or Christological shape or grounding of this experience?'), or with a text ('What does Barth say about this?'). Rather, they begin with a sustained focus on the conditions, qualities, and implications of the experience.

This is a phenomenological and hermeneutical habit. Phenomenology and hermeneutics ask about the ways experience is constituted: how we identify and relate to the objects of our enquiry, how they affect us and we them, and how these relationships change and interact with others.[27]

Theology, it seems to me, both demands and complicates such questions because God is not simply an object of enquiry. As Kierkegaard showed so meticulously, humans' relations with God are necessarily subjective and personal because God defies objectification.[28] On the one hand, therefore, to assume an 'objective', disengaged standpoint from which to investigate God's existence and character misses an essential part of what one seeks to understand, namely that there is no such standpoint. On the other, asking these questions in relation to God reveals God as a *transformative* subject matter which directly affects our vision not only of the world, but of ourselves, our modes of knowledge, and how we are to live, act, and speak in the world. This does not leave phenomenology or hermeneutics untouched. The aim of this book, therefore, is neither a pure phenomenology nor a systematic theology, but a mixed account that reflects the depth, breadth, and complexity of ordinary and intellectual life, especially a life of faith.

The Plan of This Book

The work of this book unfolds in five chapters. Following the introductory Chapter 1, Chapter 2 begins by interrogating the modern ideal of authenticity, which has arisen in partial response to the loss of inherited confidence in objective metaphysical and moral frameworks. I argue that by assuming an unmediated access to an 'authentic' self, this ideal fails to acknowledge the ways in which even our self-understanding is mediated by imaginative projections that are never purely personal but always inherited and constructed. These complex, communal dynamics of our imaginative construal of selfhood are not to be evaded but, rather, engaged. I therefore discuss role-playing – the inhabitation of social and narrative roles – as indispensable for forming authentic relationships to oneself and others. Such role-playing exemplifies both the risks and the possibilities of imaginative finding and making, and though it does not solve the problem of self-understanding, it elucidates its limits. Drawing on meta-theatrical examples from William Shakespeare and Samuel Beckett, I argue for a creative and open-ended life with roles.

Chapter 3 extends the argument of Chapter 2 by describing language itself as an inherited practice of imaginative gestalt formation, shaping an inarticulate 'mess of imprecision of feeling' (T. S. Eliot) into inherited forms of verbal sense-making. This practice is always necessarily fraught with ambiguity. The underdetermination of the stuff that is shaped into language is neither conclusively resolved by articulation nor available in more direct, unmediated form. The patterns into which it is cast are neither fully stable nor fully shared among conversation partners. The resulting ambiguity of all our speaking is constitutive of our common life with language; yet we inhabit it, for the most part, unaware of our own role in it. I argue that the verbal experiments of poetry bring this dynamic to consciousness and create new possibilities of inhabiting the world in language.

I then widen this argument to other forms of art, showing how visual artists loosen our habituated ways of encountering the visible world by bringing to consciousness our own imaginative work of seeing. In doing so, artists do not impose an alternative picture of the world (as if making could, after all, be reduced to finding) but rather grant us a double vision that allows us to see the world in new ways, consciously participating in its utterance. The chapter concludes by discussing ways in which the Christian liturgy and Scriptures enable such renewals of perception in more existentially demanding ways.

Chapter 4 investigates this theological claim critically by examining the imaginative work that goes into a life with God. I draw on psychological research and on the spiritual senses tradition to discuss the malleability of the human sense of God, suggesting both the power of spiritual formation and the unavoidable risk of projection and self-deception. I then discuss how, in the case of spiritual realities that are acknowledged to be beyond material presence, it is possible to speak about 'perception' at all: whether there can be signs or criteria. Drawing on C. S. Lewis's theory of transposition, and on the foregoing discussion of art, I discuss ways in which an imaginative perception of a 'metaphysical depth' beyond the physical order might be possible. I conclude by emphasizing the centrality of an experience of divine absence, and of the nonsensicality rather than merely the meaningfulness of the world, to such spiritual vision.

The end of Chapter 4 moves from phenomenological to theological argument, and Chapter 5 concludes that turn, laying out a theological account of eschatology and arguing for ways in which the human experience of finding and making is consonant and can be lived in light of it. Christian eschatology affirms a divine purpose for creation, which invites humans into creative co-creation. At the same time, it promises the consummation of this purpose not as the actualization of latent potential but as a divine gift of new creation. This promise is both an invitation to imagine the world differently and a declaration of the limits of all imaginative construction. Drawing again on Shakespeare and Beckett, I outline a form of theatre that exhibits what I call an eschatological imagination. The concluding Chapter 6 suggests the significance of such an eschatological imagination within ordinary life.

Together, these chapters argue that if the Christian faith is a way of making sense of the world, it does not do so merely by laying out a metaphysical or doctrinal pattern to which to adjust our perception. Rather, it makes sense of the world by enabling us to hold open horizons that we always rush to foreclose, and to sustain uncertainty in the light of a divine promise. To realize this capacity, however, requires a deep faith in a God whom we cannot grasp and take full hold of: a God who is not simply available and who does not simply enable the fulfilment of our ambitions, though he holds out the gift of eternal life. Such faith engenders, among other things, a self-abnegating theological imagination: a realization of both the adequacy and inadequacy of our ways of sense-making to the mystery of creation. Yes, theology constructs. It constructs metaphysical accounts of the world; it constructs theories and images to guide us. But they are light, tentative, humble, because when we construct theologically, we are not building towers; we are building boats. And we trust the sea.

Notes

1. The history of the term *Einbildungskraft* or *imagination* is indicative of, though not coextensive with, the phenomenon this book has in view. That phenomenon is described in a variety of terms and accounts, some of which are discussed later in the Chapter 1. Already Thomas Aquinas, following Aristotle, gives a related account centred on the concept of the *conversio ad phantasmata* in *Summa Theologiae* 1.86.2 and 2; 1.84.7; see Aquinas, *Summa Theologiae: Latin Text and English Translation, Introductions, Notes, Appendices, and Glossaries*, translated and edited Thomas Gilby et al., 61 vols (London: Blackfriars in conjunction with Eyre & Spottiswoode, 1964–1981). There is, to my knowledge, neither a full history of the manifold accounts of the constructive or creative aspect of human perception (what this book calls 'imagination') nor of the term 'imagination' in its manifold uses; but see e.g. Mary Warnock, *Imagination* (London: Faber, 1976); Edward S. Casey, *Imagining: A Phenomenological Study* (Indianapolis: Indiana University Press, 1976).

   The term 'imagination' as used in this book is indebted primarily to the continental tradition of philosophy. There has also been a growing interest in the imagination in the analytic tradition, which is engendering scholarship whose sources, questions, assumptions, and methods often differ from those of the continental scholarship on either the term or the phenomenon. This book does not engage directly with this growing analytic literature, which is represented e.g. by Shaun Nichols (ed.), *The Architecture of the Imagination: New Essays on Pretense, Possibility, and Fiction* (Oxford: Oxford University Press, 2006); Tamar Szabó Gendler, *Intuition, Imagination, and Philosophical Methodology* (Oxford: Oxford University

Press, 2010); Amy Kind (ed.), *The Routledge Handbook of Philosophy of Imagination* (London: Routledge, 2016); Amy Kind and Peter Kung (eds), *Knowledge through Imagination* (Oxford: Oxford University Press, 2016); Kathleen Stock, *Only Imagine: Fiction, Interpretation and Imagination* (Oxford: Oxford University Press, 2017); Greg Currie, *Imagining and Knowing: The Shape of Fiction* (Oxford: Oxford University Press, 2020); Amy Kind and Christopher Badura (eds), *Epistemic Uses of Imagination* (London: Routledge, 2021); Amy Kind, *Imagination and Creative Thinking* (Cambridge: Cambridge University Press, 2022).

2. Warnock, *Imagination*, 10.

3. David Hume, *A Treatise of Human Nature*, edited by David Fate Norton and Mary J. Norton (Oxford: Clarendon Press, 2000), 1.1.7.15. On Hume's concept of imagination, see e.g. J. Broughton, 'Impressions and Ideas,' in S. Traiger (ed.), *The Blackwell Guide to Hume's Treatise* (Oxford: Blackwell, 2006), 43–58; T. M. Costelloe, *The Imagination in Hume's Philosophy* (Edinburgh: Edinburgh University Press, 2018); Tito Magri, *Hume's Imagination* (Oxford: Oxford University Press, 2022).

4. Immanuel Kant, *Kritik der reinen Vernunft* (Riga: Harknoch, edition A 1781, edition B 1787), translated and edited by Paul Guyer and Allen W. Wood as *Critique of Pure Reason* (Cambridge: Cambridge University Press, 1999), A141 = B181. The imagination (*Einbildungskraft*) is a central concept in Kant's account of the possibility of experience and understanding, and there is a great deal of scholarship on the topic, including Karl Homann, 'Zum Begriff Einbildungskraft nach Kant,' *Archiv für Begriffsgeschichte* 14 (1970), 266–302; Hermann Mörchen, *Die Einbildungskraft bei Kant* (Berlin: de Gruyter, 1970); Rudolf Makkreel, *Imagination and Interpretation in Kant* (Chicago, IL: University of Chicago Press,

1990); Gary Banham, *Kant's Transcendental Imagination* (London: Palgrave Macmillan, 2005); Jane Kneller, *Kant and the Power of Imagination* (Cambridge: Cambridge University Press, 2007); Matthias Wunsch, *Einbildungskraft und Erfahrung bei Kant* (Berlin: de Gruyter, 2012); Michael L. Thompson (ed.), *Imagination in Kant's Critical Philosophy* (Berlin: De Gruyter, 2016); Rolf-Peter Horstmann, *Kant's Power of Imagination* (Cambridge: Cambridge University Press, 2018); Timothy Burns et al. (eds), *The New Yearbook for Phenomenology and Phenomenological Philosophy*, vol. 17, pt 2: *The Imagination: Kant's Phenomenological Legacy* (London: Routledge, 2019).

5. Exemplary philosophical treatments of faces are Stanley Cavell, 'Knowing and Acknowledging,' in *Must We Mean What We Say?* (Cambridge: Cambridge University Press, 1969), 238–266; Roger Scruton, *The Face of God* (London: Continuum, 2014); Hans Belting, *Face and Mask: A Double History*, translated by Thomas S. Hansen and Abby J. Hansen (Princeton, NJ: Princeton University Press, 2017). Empirical studies show that those suffering from depression or schizophrenia have a greater tendency to see and remember faces as displaying negative affect; see e.g. Jukka M. Leppänen, Maarten Milders, J. Stephen Bell, Emma Terriere, and Jari K. Hietanen, 'Depression Biases the Recognition of Emotionally Neutral Faces,' *Psychiatry Research* 128, no. 2 (2004), 123–133; Sara M. Levens and Ian H. Gotlib, 'Updating Positive and Negative Stimuli in Working Memory in Depression,' *Journal of Experimental Psychology: General* 139, no. 4 (2010), 654–664; A. E. Pinkham, C. Brensinger, C. Kohler, R. E. Gur, and R. C. Gur, 'Actively Paranoid Patients with Schizophrenia Over-Attribute Anger to Neutral Faces,' *Schizophrenia Research* 125, nos. 2–3 (2011), 174–178.

6. 'L'imagination dispose de tout. Elle fait la beauté, la justice et le bonheur qui est le tout du monde'; Pascal, *Pensées*, edited by Philippe Sellier (Paris: Garnier, 1999), 78. Pascal's concept of imagination does not, of course, wholly overlap with mine; examinations of his concept are found e.g. in Gérard Ferreyrolles, *Les reines du monde: l'imagination et la coutume chez Pascal* (Paris: Champion, 1995); Matthew Maguire, *The Conversion of Imagination: From Pascal through Rousseau to Tocqueville* (Cambridge, MA: Harvard University Press, 2006); Alberto Frigo, 'Necessary Error: Pascal on Imagination and Descartes's Fourth Meditation,' *Early Modern French Studies* 39, no. 1 (2017), 31–44.

7. S. T. Coleridge, *Biographia Literaria or Biographical Sketches of My Literary Life and Opinions*, edited by James Engell and W. Jackson Bate (Princeton, NJ: Princeton University Press, 1983), 1:304 (ch. 13). The literature on Coleridge's and Romantic thought on the imagination is vast. Classic studies include I. A. Richards, *Coleridge on Imagination* (London: Kegan Paul, Trench, Trubner & Co, 1934); J. Robert Barth, *The Symbolic Imagination: Coleridge and the Romantic Tradition* (Princeton, NJ: Princeton University Press, 1977).

8. Ernst Gombrich, *Art and Illusion* (London: Phaedon, 2nd ed., 1961), 145–231.

9. Maurice Merleau-Ponty, *Phénomènologie de la perception* (Paris: Gallimard, 1945), translated by Colin Smith as *The Phenomenology of Perception* (London: Routledge, 1962), xxiv.

10. See e.g. the collection of Max Wertheimer's writings in W. D. Ellis (ed.), *A Source Book of Gestalt Psychology* (London: Kegan Paul, Trench, Trubner & Co, 1938); Ludwig Wittgenstein, *Philosophical Investigations = Philosophische Untersuchungen*, edited and translated by G. E. M.

Anscombe (Oxford: Blackwell, 1953), pt 2, §xi; Merleau-Ponty, *Phenomenology of Perception*. The clearest account of the wider significance of Wittgenstein's discussion of aspect perception or seeing-as remains Stephen Mulhall, *On Being in the World: Wittgenstein and Heidegger on Seeing Aspects* (London: Routledge, 1990).

11. See, for example, the literature on the Stroop effect.

12. An eighteen-month project entitled *Mapping the Imagination*, funded by the Templeton Religion Trust (TRT0354) at the University of St Andrews, investigated just such mutual challenges, questions, and illuminations. The project was led by Prof. Judith Wolfe in collaboration with Dr Marina Iosifyan and produced a range of empirical studies, presented among others in Marina Iosifyan, Anton Sidoroff-Dorso, and Judith Wolfe, 'Cross-Modal Associations between Paintings and Sounds: Effects of Embodiment,' *Perception* 51, no. 12 (2023), 871–888; Marina Iosifyan and Judith Wolfe, 'Everyday Life vs Art: Effects of Perceptual Context on the Mode of Object Interpretation,' *Empirical Studies of the Arts* 42, no. 1 (2023), 166–191; Marina Iosifyan and Judith Wolfe, 'Buffering Effect of Fiction on Negative Emotions: Engagement with Negatively Valenced Fiction Decreases the Intensity of Negative Emotions,' *Cognition and Emotion* (2024): 1–18, doi: https://doi.org/10.1080/02699931.2024.2314986; and Marina Iosifyan and Judith Wolfe, 'Poetry vs Everyday Life: Context Increases Perceived Meaningfulness of Sentences' (under review).

13. The best introduction to predictive processing remains Andy Clark, *Surfing Uncertainty* (Oxford: Oxford University Press, 2016). Though sometimes criticized as relying on a representational model of perception and cognition by other theorists of enactive, embedded, embodied, and extended (4E)

cognition, many predictive processing theorists (incl. Clark) rely on embodied cognition; for discussions, see e.g. M. Miller and A. Clark, 'Happily Entangled: Prediction, Emotion, and the Embodied Mind,' *Synthese* 195 (2018), 2559–2575; Jakob Hohwy, 'The Predictive Processing Hypothesis,' in Albert Newen, Leon De Bruin, and Shaun Gallagher (eds), *The Oxford Handbook of 4E Cognition* (Oxford: Oxford University Press, 2018), 129–146. I have written briefly about the relationship of my philosophical questions and predictive processing in Judith Wolfe, 'The Renewal of Perception in Religious Faith and Biblical Narrative,' *European Journal for Philosophy of Religion* 13, no. 4 (2022), 111–128.

14. The term 'metaphysical dream' was coined by Richard Weaver in *Ideas Have Consequences* (Chicago, IL: University of Chicago Press, 1948), 17 and *passim*.

15. Kant, *Critique of Pure Reason* A78 = B103; see also A120.

16. Warnock, *Imagination*, 25.

17. Jean-François Lyotard, *La Condition postmoderne: Rapport sur le savoir* (Paris: Éditions de Minuit, 1979), translated by Geoffrey Bennington and Brian Massumi as *The Postmodern Condition: A Report on Knowledge* (Minneapolis: University of Minnesota Press, 1984); Michel Foucault, *Les mots et les choses: Une archéologie des sciences humaines* (Paris: Gallimard, 1966), translated as *The Order of Things* (New York: Pantheon, 1970); Foucault, *L'Archéologie du Savoir* (Paris: Gallimard, 1969), translated by A. M. Sheridan Smith as *The Archaeology of Knowledge* (New York: Pantheon, 1972); Gilles Deleuze and Félix Guattari, *Capitalisme et schizophrénie. L'anti-Œdipe* (Paris: Les Éditions de Minuit, 1972), translated by Robert Hurley, Mark Seem, and Helen R. Lane as *Anti-Oedipus* (Minneapolis, MN: University of Minnesota Press, 1972); Judith Butler, *Gender Trouble:*

Feminism and the Subversion of Identity (New York: Routledge, 1990) and *Bodies That Matter: On the Discursive Limits of 'Sex'* (New York: Routledge, 1993).

18. See Yuval Noah Harari in *Sapiens: A Brief History of Humankind* (London: Vintage, 2014) and *Homo Deus: A Brief History of Tomorrow* (London: Vintage, 2016).

19. A recent work arguing the complementary converse of my case – namely that images have their own power to instil in us an 'incomprehensible certainty' of the world's metaphysical depth – is Thomas Pfau, *Incomprehensible Certainty: Metaphysics and Hermeneutics of the Image* (South Bend, IN: Notre Dame University Press, 2022).

20. This is a central claim of theorists of predictive processing, as well as influential strands of analytic philosophy (e.g. Willard Van Orman Quine, 'Two Dogmas of Empiricism,' *The Philosophical Review* 60 (1951), 20–43).

21. See e.g. Susie Hodge, *Why Your Five Year Old Could Not Have Done That: Modern Art Explained* (London: Thames & Hudson, 2012).

22. The Ames Room is named after its inventor, Adelbert Ames, who constructed the first such room in 1946 on principles derived from Hermann Helmholtz; see W. H. Ittelson, *The Ames Demonstrations in Perception* (London and Princeton, NJ: Hafner, 1952). Much research has been conducted with and on this visual experiment, and there are conflicting accounts of its implications. A seminal debate is that between James J. Gibson (in *The Senses Considered as Perceptual Systems* (London: Allen & Unwin, 1966) and subsequent works) and Ernst H. Gombrich (in *Art and Illusion*). The so-called Honi phenomenon, named after the woman who first reported it, shows that very close familiarity with a person in the Ames Room will sometimes override its effect;

see seminally Warren J. Wittreich, 'The Honi Phenomenon: A Case of Selective Perceptual Distortion,' *Journal of Abnormal & Social Psychology* 47, no. 3 (July 1952), 705–712; Kenneth L. and Karen K. Dion, 'The Honi Phenomenon Revisited: Factors Underlying the Resistance to Perceptual Distortion of One's Partner,' *Journal of Personality and Social Psychology* 33, no. 2 (1976), 170–177.

23. Stanley Cavell, 'Music Discomposed,' in *Must We Mean What We Say?*, 180–212, p. 188.

24. Although I will later discuss some points of specifically Christian doctrine, I will not offer any direct comparison of Christian theological resources with those of other religions or explicitly delimit Christian faith against other faiths. How other religious traditions agree and differ in their approaches to the questions raised in this book is for practitioners of those traditions to answer.

25. Thomas Aquinas, *Summa Theologiae* 1.1.7. See also esp. John Webster, 'What Makes Theology Theological?' in *God without Measure: Working Papers in Christian Theology* (London: T&T Clark, 2016), vol. 1, ch. 14, and 'Theological Theology,' in *Confessing God: Essays in Christian Dogmatics II* (London: Bloomsbury T&T Clark, 2016), ch. 1.

26. Chris Insole makes this case in detail in *Negative Natural Theology* (Oxford: Oxford University Press, 2025).

27. A good introduction to phenomenology is Robert Sokolowski, *Introduction to Phenomenology* (Cambridge: Cambridge University Press, 1999). Since the beginning of phenomenology in the early twentieth century, the relation between phenomenology and metaphysics – whether phenomenology bars, presupposes, implies, or fleshes out metaphysics, or exposes any attempt at metaphysics as incoherent – has been a central topic of debate. Edmund

Husserl and Martin Heidegger were both ambivalent about the question and adopted changing views on it; and the extent to which, independently of their explicit thoughts on the question, their own phenomenologies were metaphysically implicated is very much a living debate. For their own views, see Husserl, *Die Krisis der europäischen Wissenschaften und die transzendentale Phänomenologie: Eine Einleitung in die phänomenologische Philosophie* (The Hague: Martinus Nijhoff, 1954), translated by David Carr as *The Crisis of European Sciences and Transcendental Phenomenology: An Introduction to Phenomenological Philosophy* (Evanston, IL: Northwestern University Press, 1970) and other works; and Heidegger, *Sein und Zeit* (Halle: Niemeyer, 1927), translated by John Macquarrie and Edward Robinson as *Being and Time* (Oxford: Blackwell, 1962). For early debates, see esp. Edith Stein, 'Husserls Phänomenologie und die Philosophie des Hl. Thomas von Aquino,' in Martin Heidegger (ed.), *Festschrift, Edmund Husserl zum 70. Geburtstag gewidmet* (Halle: Niemeyer, 1929), 315–338, and Erich Przywara, 'Drei Richtungen der Phänomenologie,' *Stimmen der Zeit* 115 (1928), 252–264. Recent contributions include Stefano Bancalari (ed.), *Religion et 'Attitude Naturelle', Archivio di Filosofia* 90, nos. 2–3 (2022); Judith Wolfe, *Heidegger and Theology* (London: T&T Clark, 2014); and many others. The debate surrounding later phenomenology, particularly the second and third generation of French phenomenologists, was seminally shaped by Dominique Janicaud (ed.), *Le Tournant théologique de la phénoménologie française* (Combas: Éditions de l'Éclat, 1991), translated as *Phenomenology and the Theological Turn: The French Debate* (New York: Fordham University Press, 2001).

28. See e.g. Kierkegaard, *Begrebet Angest: En simpel psychologisk-paapegende Overveielse i Retning af det dogmatiske* (Copenhagen: C. A. Reitzel, 1843), translated by Reidar Thomte as *The Concept of Anxiety* (Princeton, NJ: Princeton University Press, 1980); Kierkegaard, *Sygdommen til Døden: En christelig psychologisk Udvikling til Opbyggelse og Opvækkelse* (Copenhagen: C. A. Reitzel, 1849), translated by Edna H. Hong and Howard V. Hong as *The Sickness unto Death* (Princeton, NJ: Princeton University Press, 1983).

2 | Making Up a Life

And even if grey drafts of emptiness
blow from the stage,
I yet remain.

Rilke, 'Fourth Duino Elegy'

Narrating Ourselves

I have argued in Chapter 1 that the work of perception is mostly hidden from us: that we usually experience ourselves as merely finding the world, rather than as participating in making it. We are rarely aware either of the continual activity of shaping underdetermined impressions into patterns, or of the malleability of these patterns by the influences with which we surround ourselves. This is true not only of our understanding of the world that surrounds us, but also of our understanding of ourselves.

Charles Guignon tells the story of the Reformation and its aftermath (imprecisely but evocatively) as a story of disillusionment with authority as a guide to good order, and an inward turn towards conscience and personal faith, fuelled by a belief that the presence of God can be found in the core of our selves. Gradually, Guignon recounts, the idea of God fell away, and we were left with a faith in an inner deity, an inner core of authentic selfhood: and if only we could find and be true to that inner self, hidden independently of social obligations and roles at the heart of our own being, then we would have access to what defines truth and goodness, and be 'true selves'.[1]

But the suggestion at the heart of this ideal of authenticity – that there might be a self to be found that is unmediated by roles or constructions – is unrealistic. Rather, the self is accessed and lived out in the form of an unfolding, but also constantly re-narrated, story about ourselves. One might say, indeed, that telling a story about our own lives, projecting a whole out of its parts, is a primary work of the human imagination. We cannot understand or grasp ourselves apart from telling our story, a coherent narrative in which we ourselves are the protagonist. In this process, there is a strange dynamic at work: for the creation of our story often feels to us supremely like a work of *finding* – of unearthing our true story, and thereby making sense of our lives – while it is also, undeniably, a work of *construction*. By construction I do not mean merely that we create the story of our lives by living it: of course it is, amid everything else, our choices and actions that shape the story we live. By 'construction' I here mean, rather, the ways in which we narrate our past to inform our present choices and our future possibilities. In order to have a moral space in which to move in the present and future, we have to *believe* in the story we tell about our past; otherwise, it cannot serve as an orienting framework. And yet (mostly unconsciously), this telling is a work of the form-giving imagination, which selects from the myriad and ever-shifting data points a narrative pattern. We can see the cracks of its reality or objectivity when we come to crisis points that force us to re-narrate our past: a radical failure, a disillusionment, a break-up. And yet even then, the emotional force of the re-narration will usually be one of *discovery* rather than *construction*: 'This, finally, is the truth of my life.' Until the next crisis.

Psychology has vital things to say about the importance of narrating our lives to achieve and maintain a healthy self. Narrative therapy is based on the insight that the experiences we cannot narrate are often those that control us; that severe trauma is so debilitating partly because it makes it impossible to tell a coherent story about ourselves; that narrating our story is a form of taking hold of it, of inhabiting it consciously rather than unwittingly, and therefore of liberation. All this is true and important. But it often comes at the cost of pretending that our story is something we find more receptively, construe less actively, than is in fact the case. This has multiple risks. The first is that the more we insist on our individual stories, the less aware we often are of how conventional the roles we take are, and of how influenced we are by the narrative models touted by the latest films, books, or influencers. What feels like authenticity is often mere cliché. The second is that ignorance of how much our stories rely on the active selection and interpretation of nodal points and events makes us rigid, and often crowds out other perspectives and people. In particular, they force other people into roles within our narrative, selecting and matching their actions to a pattern that makes sense within the plot unfolding in *our* mind. But our narrative roles are always, in some basic sense, incommensurate with one another. We are always the *protagonists* of our own lives, and cast others in roles vis-à-vis ourselves with which they (almost by definition) cannot themselves fully identify: supporting or antagonistic roles. Of course we acknowledge, at least in theory, that others, too, are protagonists to themselves; but it is something of which we need continually to remind ourselves. Conversely, what role we play in one another's consciousness is often beyond our knowledge and certainly beyond our control.

This dynamic can lead to profound loneliness and disorientation. Charles Taylor's condition of the 'buffered self'[2] has been intensified in nearly unimaginable ways in the new habits of digital interaction embedded by the Covid-19 pandemic. Online meetings connect us, but radically change our sense of presence. They allow us to reduce each other to squares on our own screens, to be pinned, shifted, minimized, muted, and turned off at will. To some extent, they actively realize the vision of the world played out in Descartes' *Meditations* (or in a darkened theatre): we are no longer corporeal persons in a shared space, whose relative movements affect one another, but apparitions slotted into plays or stories that are increasingly of each one's solitary imagining.[3] The more we insist on the role of protagonist and cast others into supporting or antagonistic roles, the more we manoeuvre ourselves into competition or worse, find ourselves the only players among non-player characters in a cosmos without coordinates.

What does all this have to do with theology? To some extent, the simple answer is that it is an axiom of theology that we are not the ultimate tellers of the stories of our lives; that our lives are, indeed, part of a larger story, in which we do not have to be perfect protagonists, but are, as sinners who are loved by God, forgiven and restored to a story in which love places *all* at the centre and *all* at the service of all others. C. S. Lewis captures this powerfully not only in the great dance that concludes *Perelandra*, but above all in *Till We Have Faces*, in which the story Orual tells about herself crumbles in her hands and runs through her fingers. It is only when she is told her own story by a god that she, too, can be Psyche, *soul*; that her story turns out to be intertwined, redemptively, with the stories of those she has loved but has wounded and lost. This may well be the form that the Last Judgement will take: this retelling of our stories that integrates them into a larger story of love. It is our fervent hope that this will be so.

But while we await that judgment, we live in a world in which we cannot escape our own imagination, both individual and collective; in which our imagining of ourselves and others is at once inescapable, inadequate, and often mutually incommensurate. This is true even of our place within the Christian story, insofar as we accept it. Though the Christian story of creation, fall, and redemption is genuinely larger than we are, it is nevertheless to some extent our responsibility to locate ourselves within it narratively, and we can get entangled in our own telling. (Talk to anyone who has had a major crisis of faith or life and looks back with puzzlement and disappointment on the way she has been telling her own spiritual story. This is one of the reasons why liturgy and community are so very important.)

41

Our *practical* work may well be, above all, to sit lightly to our imagining: to be willing constantly to revise our own narratives in light of the gospel, of new evidence, and of the presence of others. But this is no easy thing to do. It is indispensable, therefore, to think critically and reflectively about the imaginative work involved in constructing roles and narratives, here between the times.

Role-Playing

I have been talking about the narrative roles that we assign ourselves and others in the stories we constantly tell – in our heads and often increasingly on social media – about our lives. But these are not the only type of roles that structure our lives: there is another life-structuring type of role which I will call 'social roles'. Although also a matter of imagination in my sense, social roles are a product of the *collective* imagination of a society more than of any individual imagination. They are roles that originate within a social web and which we inherit and perform, in some sense, communally and in public. These roles vary greatly in their scope and perdurance: some last a lifetime while others come and go; some can be combined while others are mutually exclusive. There are biologically grounded and enduring roles such as child, sister, or mother; status-defined roles such as benefactor or patron; life-stage-specific roles such as pupil, student, or pensioner; professional roles such as accountant, teacher, or plumber; and the shifting and varied roles of friend, lover, volunteer, or hobby sportsman. All these are defined not individually but socially, by their position within a social web; they are communally positioned, communally passed on, and at least to some extent publicly available. They are therefore, in all their variety, rightly called social roles.

To offer a critical appreciation of social roles within an account of the irreversibility of the modern condition seems at first counter-intuitive precisely because the older, irretrievable ideal of a fixed moral order was often acted out through equally fixed, socially indexed roles. To be a good citizen or a good Christian was to step into social roles that prescribed frameworks of behaviour and excellence: squire, clerk, *pater familias*, servant. Those who were subordinate within the overarching order also had to accept subordinate roles in society. In the emancipatory climate of Western modernity, social roles were therefore increasingly seen as instruments of oppression: inflexible moulds pressed down on inner lives in stifling and unfairly stratifying ways. Kierkegaard associates this kind of role play with an inauthentic 'Christendom' that stands over against an authentic 'Christianity'. Heidegger associates it with 'das Man' – the tyranny of the impersonal 'they'.[4]

But what are social roles? In practice, they are behavioural patterns that have developed over long periods of trial and error to enable and maximize certain aims or values. It could be said that roles are some of the key forms in which societies find, negotiate, and pursue their goods. What is passed on with a role is a whole complex of implicit knowledge about social goods (in this sense of aims and values) and how to realize them, codified in patterns of behaviour whose purpose no individual may fully understand but which he or she can nevertheless help realize. Roles, in other words, pass on possibilities of comportment and movement within the world, and allow one to achieve certain modes of excellence. For example, I have inherited the role of university professor. This role comes with agreed privileges and obligations, agreed patterns of behaviour that include practices which would seem strange or rude in a different context. If I returned a letter from a friend with the same brisk red annotations with which I habitually fill my students' essays, she would likely resent me. Yet this practice is accepted as conducive to the characteristic goods of a university: education and the pursuit of knowledge and truth.

This means that social roles also represent risks and temptations. They are neither immutable nor 'safe'. On one side of the spectrum, they can be means of codifying and justifying exploitative behaviour. On the other, they can develop their own dynamics and run away from any consciously chosen purposes. (Take, for example, the social media influencer, a role arising in part from the artificial reward mechanisms of social media, which create patterns of behaviour whose consequences we do not yet comprehend.) The deep anxiety and contestation surrounding the way teachers, pastors, and parents should act – what their responsibilities and privileges are – reflects a profound communal uncertainty about the meaning of the values their institutions exist to pursue.

Even when they are relatively stable structures for the pursuit of certain goods, roles are optimized for what works best in the aggregate: individual situations might call for different responses or actions. For this reason, the notion of a 'virtuoso', familiar from the arts, is relevant also to social roles: A virtuoso is capable of mastering or internalizing a role, but also of improvising, and thereby extending its range of possibilities without distorting its purpose.

Despite their risks and limitations, roles can be spaces of freedom and exploration precisely because they are at once load-bearing and malleable. Amid the profound anxiety of our age, it can seem impossible to take hold of one overarching good by which we might orient our lives. But we can understand ourselves and each other under particular *descriptions*, that is, in particular roles: daughter and sister; pupil and friend; student; worker; parent. Many of these roles are rooted in physical realities but are also associated with characteristic goods and virtues. They give us spaces for action; within them, we can achieve excellence and meaning. Our roles, though we often assume them deliberately, in an important sense also precede us: they are, in some ways, bigger than we and can become moulds into which we can pour our liquid selves. In role-playing of this sort, the anxiety of authenticity falls, at least for a while, legitimately away: sincerity *follows* rather than motivates choice. In that sense, it is more important to choose the right role than to strive for authenticity. As Kurt Vonnegut said: 'We are what we pretend to be, so we must be careful about what we pretend to be.'[5]

Charles Taylor talks about inescapable frameworks of moral action.[6] In practice, within the global horizon of the dialectic of life and death, our frameworks are mostly defined not globally but by social roles. My values are those of a mother, a wife, a scholar, a member of certain communities. It is within these roles that certain things count as goods or as non-negotiable conditions: it is as a mother that I delight in the flourishing of these children and that my allegiance to them is non-negotiable. It is as a scholar that I derive satisfaction from a well-given lecture or a well-received article, and that commitment to certain kinds of truth is non-negotiable. Roles, as I said, are scripts of behaviour for the realization of certain goods, and it is the attainment of these goods that makes us happy. Likewise, it is when we find ourselves incapable of realizing the goods of a particular role or when we cannot derive joy from them that we experience existential crises.

These descriptions also suggest a dimension that is perhaps less immediately obvious but equally important to our consideration of roles as ways of inhabiting the world well. Roles not only create spaces for action, attainment, and delight; they also delimit our obligations. 'What do we owe others?' is an intensely fraught question in philosophy and literature: Emmanuel Levinas dogmatically resolves it in favour of infinite responsibility; Stanley Cavell never comes to transparent terms with it; Rowan Williams, following Hegel, sees it as one of the basic themes of tragic drama.[7]

A common answer is that we owe others whatever we have incurred by debt or bindingly undertaken to give. But even if this is so, we immediately have to add that such undertakings only *sometimes* take the form of explicit promises ('I vow to avenge you') or concrete debts ('I owe you my life'). More often, they arise as part of contracts and scripts between social roles which we enter with more or less consciousness as we make use of their forms. In other words, we seldom merely act; we take on actions that pertain to certain roles. And we seldom merely speak; we use language that is part of particular patterns (whether long established or newly defined by current literature and other media). And these roles and patterns always have a *scope* that extends beyond singular action. Indeed, we might say that roles are, among other things, long-calibrated patterns of mutual obligation and privilege, scripted ways of fulfilling each other's needs and our own. (Painful crises in life arise when we are in a role which comes with an obligation to fulfil needs which we as individuals are not, however, capable of fulfilling.)

Cavell and Levinas both suggest that as soon as we see the humanity of someone, we (should) realize that there is no limit to our obligation towards them. This is true, but unliveable. Roles give us a framework to *delimit obligation* and to do so legitimately. This does not, of course, let us off the hook. Choices regarding what roles to assume and how much scope to grant them are themselves (at least sometimes) our responsibility; and some calls transcend the boundaries of our roles. Similarly, that different roles may create conflicting obligations is one of the central themes of ancient tragedy. In Shakespeare's tragic canon, the dilemma is well dramatized in *Romeo and Juliet*, where Juliet's obligations as daughter and as lover are in literally deadly conflict. The conflict raises the difficult question of the relative claims of role-internal obligations and the right or obligation of assuming or relinquishing roles in the first place. The question, in Juliet's case, is *both* what she owes Romeo as his betrothed *and how* to assess the legitimacy of assuming that role. Her antecedent role as daughter of the House of Capulet precludes it; and this raises the difficult question, never to be answered by rote, of the scope of that former role. If she assumes a role that conflicts with another, should she relinquish the first or should she remain committed to as much of it as she can, bearing the constant conflict this will create for her and others?

Once relinquished, a role's internal obligations cease with it (which is why it can be so liberating to shed a role). At the same time, this sometimes comes at the price of the incalculable debt or burden – incalculable in the strict sense that there is no agreed calculus for it – of having abandoned the role in the first place. Sometimes, the limit or end of a role is scripted into the role itself: the end of a term of office; the passing of the baton to another; mutual agreement. But often, it does violence to oneself or others. Once one has broken up with a romantic partner, one no longer has the obligation or privilege to console her; but how is one to calculate the responsibility for acquiring that lack of responsibility in the first place? It is beyond the contracts of one's roles.[8]

On the one hand, therefore, obligations are mediated (except in very concrete, specific circumstances) by social roles which together make up a social compact, though by no means a coherent or unified one: obligations accrue to roles which do not always cohere with other sets of roles. Obligations are, in that sense, not matters of our choosing, control, or even surveyability, though to perform a role well just means to know and shoulder its obligations, which makes one, as Katherine Hawley argued, trustworthy.[9]

On the other hand, there are always ambiguities in the obligations that accrue to our role-playing. These arise, above all, at the beginning and end of role-playing: in the questions how to assess the legitimacy of assuming a role (think of Juliet's betrothal) and relinquishing it (think of King Edward VIII or Pope Benedict XVI). But they arise also from the always incomplete 'fit' between self and role. Sometimes this incompleteness is a matter of capacity (Fantine may be incapable of fulfilling the role of mother) and sometimes of intention. I have said that we seldom 'merely' speak or act, but rather inhabit the patterns of certain roles whose scope exceeds individual words or acts. We often half-consciously try on roles that entail certain responsibilities, using language and gestures whose entailments we do not (and perhaps cannot) fully survey. The extent to which this use incurs the responsibilities as well as the privileges of the roles to which these words and gestures belong is often not easily arbitrated and is a frequent source of conflict and hurt. Often, there is deliberate or unintended misalignment between one person's understanding of the limits of their involvement in a social or language game and the understanding of those they speak and play with. Does flirting with Rosamond commit Lydgate to the role of suitor? Does marriage to a prince oblige a woman to a perpetually public life as princess, whether or not she understood this when she married him? This ambiguity can arise between people or within the self. If I give a homeless person food, I have done so as a single act of charity. But I also feel the pull of the fact that once I have acknowledged this as a reality *in which I play a role*, the role is not easy to shed, and may entail ongoing responsibility.

Finding the Cracks

The description in the opening section of this chapter, of (internal) *narrative* roles that go through and beyond our (external) *social* roles, may make it sound as if these ambiguities can be resolved by reliable recourse to a more constant, not role-indexed sense of self: as if we could step in and out of social roles as we can of theatrical ones. But most of the time, this is not so. Each of us has deep and distinctive instincts, needs, and desires. However, they do not congeal into an authentic self that we can access and consult apart from roles, like an oracle. It might seem like we do; but often, what we appeal to is just a different role that we are trying on for size or a narrative of selfhood that is itself malleable. Yes, we have needs and desires that run deeper than any role. But they do not themselves make up a self, though they can become paths to one. In moments in which our roles fail us, we often turn towards these needs, desires, or remoter visions that we recognize as stable or unshakeable beyond particular roles. Sometimes, it is an incontrovertible value or truth ('Whatever else may fail, nature is majestic and beautiful'). Sometimes, it is an urgent and undeniably worthy cause ('Whatever else one might do, the fight against malaria is worth dedicating oneself to'). Sometimes, it is a profound, animating desire ('Whatever else I've done, I have always wanted to paint'). Sometimes, it is the radiant reality of one other person ('Whatever else, I am made for this one'). Many great books and movies dramatize precisely such moments. But whether or not the movies show it to us (and usually they do not), the *aftermath* of these moments generally takes the shape of new roles: mountaineer, charity worker, painter, wife. And if we are lucky, those roles are precisely what roles ought to be: spaces of growth and exploration; spaces that themselves remain penultimate.

Our life with roles is so poignant because we nearly always understand ourselves 'under some description' and do not possess a dressing room away from roles where we are simply 'ourselves'. And yet, roles are also brittle and unreliable. On the one hand, roles are in some significant sense 'bigger than we': they are load-bearing structures on which we can lean and within which we can orient ourselves, seeking meaning and excellence. On the other hand, roles are always at best penultimate: within society, they are fluid, giving shape to inchoate senses of overarching meaning and value. Within lives, they display gaps, inconsistencies, tensions, which we cannot use the roles themselves to navigate. And at some point, most roles demand not fulfilment but relinquishment: our parents pass away; our children leave home; we retire from our jobs; death doth us part. Grief for our roles is also a form of grief for a lost self.

Roles, in other words, do not solve the problem of selfhood for us. However, they locate it. Shakespeare's theatre is so deeply moving partly because it harnesses the power of theatrical roles to explore the power and perplexities of the roles we play in life. Contrary to what the ideal of authenticity declares, the question of selfhood arises, when it does, most often not as the unmoored question, 'Who am I?' but in the gaps and tensions of our roleplaying. It arises when we seem too liquid to cast ourselves into any roles (as Prince Hal bemoans in *Henry IV*); when a social role we have assumed clashes with our desires (as it does for Anthony in *Anthony and Cleopatra*); when the demands of our social roles seem fundamentally ambiguous or indeterminate (as for Hamlet as the son of a Protestant father who is, impossibly, in purgatory); when the demands of two social roles clash (as they do for Hermione as wife and friend in *The Winter's Tale*); or when the internal reward structures of roles go against their wider social aim (as for Macbeth as Thane of Glamis, Thane of Cawdor, and King of Scotland).

Perhaps the most urgent and personal moments of our lives arise in the gaps and tensions within and between the roles we assume in society. Shakespeare's most arresting emblem of this is King Lear, standing on a heath in the storm that blows from just those gaps, recognizing both himself and Edgar (another inveterate role-player) for one brief moment as the same 'poor, bare, forked animal'. And yet Lear, like Shakespeare's other great characters, cannot simply stop acting. He, Hamlet, Macbeth, and Leontes all know the pathetic insufficiency of roles, but they also recognize that there is not simply a space beyond roles into which they might confidently step: Life is 'but a walking shadow, a poor player, / That struts and frets his hour upon the stage, / And then is heard no more'. 'There is no cure for that', as Samuel Beckett said.[10] When, in Shakespeare's (or Beckett's) work, characters do try to step into such a space, shedding their roles – when, perhaps, they might reach a point of authenticity beyond role-playing – why then the play is at an end.

Seeing Each Other

It is one of Stanley Cavell's great legacies to have shown that the theatre (as well as other art forms) does not merely provide illustrations or analogies for philosophical questions, but that our experiences with it can enlarge philosophical thought. This is partly because the arts, through their curious mechanisms of distillation, projection, and mirroring, allow us to see dynamics that we can never, in ordinary life, bring into focus directly, but which nevertheless inform it. Philosophers who are sensitive to these dynamics and mechanisms can examine what they could not themselves conjure. 'The conditions of theater literalize [certain] conditions [of our] existence outside', Cavell writes, and thereby effect their catharsis.[11] Thus, for example, theatrical roles embody the potential and limitation of life roles, and therefore help us to get them into view. Juliet, Hamlet, Hal, Othello, Macbeth, Hermione, Leontes, and Prospero are not mere illustrations; their multilevel existence touches and interrogates ours.[12]

This dynamic is more complex than explored so far. As I have just noted, the existence of these characters spans multiple levels; and these levels do not only echo the ordinary conditions of our own lives, but also implicate the audience, precisely in its role as audience, in ways that uncover even further conditions of selfhood. By being acted on stage, for us, theatrical characters interrogate the human need and condition of spectatorship: the extent to which selfhood is formed by the sense and reality of being seen by others. The theatre literalizes this condition and, in the hands of master playwrights, reveals its possibilities and dangers, and by creating an imaginative experience affects our life with them.

Rowan Williams remarks in *Being Human*:

> I can't think without thinking of the other. I can't even think of my body, this zero point of orientation, without understanding that it's an object to another. *I am seen*, I am heard, I am understood; and [when] I am talking about myself ... I am bound to be imagining what is not exhausted by one solitary viewpoint.[13]

The theatre has a particular way of literalizing the sense that to be a self is to be seen. For of course even in our minds, we always play for others. When we observe or experience ourselves, we see ourselves instinctively as we imagine others to be seeing us. The theatre temporarily releases its audience from this condition. It organizes shared perception in a way which in ordinary life is inescapably private, by presenting a publicly available *dramatis personae* with protagonists, supporting parts, and antagonists. In doing so, it gives us the opportunity to see figures other than ourselves as uncontested protagonists and so suspends our usual jostle for space. In the theatre, we are a real audience watching *others* as protagonists, rather than each internally watching ourselves as we imagine others (impossibly) to be watching us as protagonists. Our own role in relation to these protagonists is at once entirely marginal (we are outside their play space) and, in another sense, indispensable to the work of the play: we see the action and characters from a perspective that no one inside the play possesses, and which alone makes sense of them both.[14]

This necessity of witnesses for an achievement of under-standing is not a theatrical artefact but a condition of life. The need for recognition or acknowledgement is woven through Shakespeare's corpus, especially the late plays. Perhaps the most moving example is the once popular but now little-performed *Pericles*. Pericles, Prince of Tyre, has lost his wife and newborn daughter in a shipwreck, and has wandered the seas despairing of life. His daughter Marina, lost at sea and believed dead, was in fact found, and has been raised to a life of servitude and abuse in Mytilene. Near the end of the play, he, now an old man, harbours at Mytilene, and Marina, who has become known as one who calms and cheers others with her radiant presence, is sent to encourage him. Not knowing each other, she offers him her story: and in a poignant moment of vulnerability, it is in his hands to validate or dismiss her identity. He acknowledges her as his and is, in turn, reborn in the recognition of his daughter: 'Thou that begett'st him that did thee beget.'[15]

At first sight, it seems as if the theatre is a poor analogue to this need for recognition, precisely because there is no interaction between audience and characters. We are not in each other's lives. There is nothing we can do for one another. But this is not precisely true. Stanley Cavell argues that being an audience in a darkened theatre in fact 'literalizes' the harmful ways in which we all too often relate to each other in ordinary life (and in which the tragic protagonists Lear and Leontes relate to their own loved ones within the worlds of their plays): not by witnessing others openly, allowing them to affect us, confuse us, and change us, but by surveying them from a position of safety, commanding their presence while ourselves remaining emotionally hidden. Cavell diagnoses this attitude, which he calls 'theatricalization', as a ubiquitous defence mechanism against the existential unknowability and unavailability of the world: 'The conditions of theater literalize the conditions we exact for existence outside – hiddenness, silence, isolation – hence make that existence plain. [... I]n giving us a place within which our hiddenness and silence and separation are accounted for, it gives us a chance to stop.'[16]

Cavell's analysis of tragedic catharsis is acute but does not exhaust the richness of the metatheatrical exchange. At least in some great works of drama, being a theatre audience does not compel us to re-enact the temptation to surveil others from the dark, but brings us face to face with this temptation and gives us the chance to renounce it precisely by releasing the characters before us from their roles. This prepares us for a double movement of affirmation and renunciation which the existence of those we love demands but which is difficult to sustain or even comprehend. To acknowledge others is always both to recognize the roles they play and to confess their abiding elusiveness.

In their late plays, Shakespeare and Samuel Beckett demand such a double movement from both their characters and their audiences. The poignancy of the central figures in many of Beckett's plays, including *Endgame*, *Not I*, and especially *Play*, lies in their struggle to bring their own roles to an end. The short abstract drama *Play* presents three characters named only (with brutal stress on their stereotypicality) M, W1, and W2: a husband, his wife, and the

woman with whom he has had an affair. They are lit alter-
nately by an interrogative spotlight, which compels them to
speak. Near the end of the play, they become conscious of
the light.

> M: And now, that you are ... mere eye. Just looking. At my
> face. On and off.
> [Spot from M to W1.]
> W1: Weary of playing with me. Get off me. Yes.
> [Spot from W1 to M.]
> M: Looking for something. In my face. Some truth. In my
> eyes. Not even.
> [Spot from M to W2. Laugh as before from W2 cut short as
> spot from her to M.]
> M: Mere eye. No mind. Opening and shutting on me. Am I
> as much –
> [Spot off. Blackout. Three seconds. Spot on M.]
> M: Am I as much as ... being seen?[17]

The repeated plea for acknowledgement – 'Am I as much
as ... being seen?' – functions on multiple levels. Within
the play, it is a plea not to be reduced to a stereotype, to be
acknowledged as a person. The spotlight is an instrument
of interrogation without acknowledgement: a demand for
self-justification that repels self-disclosure. The scene echoes the trial scene in Shakespeare's *Winter's Tale*, in which
Hermione is unable to defend herself against the charge of
adultery because her husband Leontes has already cast her in
the role of adulteress and liar (here associated with the medi-
eval stock character Vice). This casting makes him deaf to
any possible defence because he can reinscribe any defence
into the role: 'I ne'er heard yet/ That any of these bolder vices

wanted/ Less impudence to gainsay what they did/ Than to perform it first.'[18] Hermione's only hope is to plead the insufficiency of the role into which her husband has locked her:

> You, my lord, best know,
> … my past life
> Hath been as continent, as chaste, as true
> As I am now unhappy, which is more
> Than history can pattern, though devised
> And played to take spectators.[19]

Hermione's plea for acknowledgement fails, and Leontes sentences her to death: a fate to which he has in some sense already condemned her in reducing her to a mere stock character. 'My life stands in the level of your dreams', she capitulates, 'which I'll lay down.'[20]

In both *Play* and *The Winter's Tale* (the generic titles are not coincidental), characters feel trapped in stock roles and plead other characters for release from those roles, for recognition as more. The theatre is an ironic place for that. After all, we know, these people only exist as roles. They are begging their interlocutors to acknowledge them as exceeding the roles in which they have been cast while we, the audience, look on as they perform their scripted roles. In *Play*, the two levels are skilfully collapsed: the interrogation spotlight is also the stage light.

What are we to do – we who have come to a theatre to watch people play roles and who are, in any case, incapacitated from action? Beckett, I think, deliberately sets us in this space to provoke us to baulk at its constriction. The actor who performs M literalizes the condition of the character: that of being trapped in a role under the watching eye of an anonymous audience. Precisely through the highly formalized, highly restrictive arrangement, he makes us see the restrictiveness of role-casting and feel the desire that there be more. 'Am I as much as being seen?' There is, in fact, nothing more to see. The character is merely M. But Beckett makes us *wish* there were.[21]

Shakespeare, more mercifully, releases us by giving us imaginative work. In *The Winter's Tale*, too, the condition of the theatre literalizes the predicament of its protagonists. We are implicated in Leontes' tyranny: it is for us that Hermione's history is 'played to take spectators'. This is why her resurrection at the end of the play is at the same time poignant and ridiculous: a miracle and theatrical hocus-pocus. The ambivalence is deliberate: we can only see her come back to life at the price of acknowledging that as long as she is on stage, we continue to trap her in a role which we must let go. The central metatheatrical puzzle of *The Winter's Tale*, whether Hermione really died or whether she hid herself, is unresolved precisely because in the theatre, they are one and the same: no one on a stage really dies. For her to rise, 'it is required [we] do awake [our] faith', in Coleridge's sense of willingly suspending our disbelief.[22] And this also means that we must be aware that that is what we are doing, and be willing to release her from her role.[23] Hermione, Puck, and Prospero plead for an acknowledgement from the audience which is at the same time their disappearance as characters. 'But release me from my bands / With the help of your good hands', says Prospero in the epilogue. 'Give me your hands if we be friends', says Puck, knowing that our acquaintance will not survive the gesture.[24] Yet our release is not simply a repudiation of roles. We are not embracing John Gielgud or Frederick Peisley as if they had finally escaped the fetters of Prospero and Puck. (In truth, we might have no interest at all in Gielgud and Peisley independently of their roles.) The trick is not to circumvent theatricality and roles, but at once to hold on and to let go: to embrace the presence granted by roles and their insufficiency.

In ordinary life, we are never an audience in the dark – we are fellow players in the lives of other people, and they in ours. But although we may not be able to step out of our own roles into a more authentic self known to us, we can recognize *others* as exceeding mere roles or as potential inhabitants of different roles; and this recognition can help them know themselves better. To display virtue and virtuosity in our lives with others means, in part, to open up possibilities for them by the ways in which we interpret their behaviour to them and give them space to develop it. There is a profound sense in which the narrative roles in which we cast *ourselves* may be less true or capacious than the possibilities created and recognition enabled by our role-playing with others. There are times and ways in which, as Stanley Cavell has insisted, others can know us better than we know ourselves.[25]

Theological Epilogue

This is a profoundly risky suggestion. It takes out of our hands any final control over the meaning of our lives and selves, suggesting that how we play into others' lives and how they see us may be equally important as our own sense of self. This seems to place into the hands of others some measure of power over that sense of self – and I am aware how much damage it can cause if people's selves are reflected back to them through twisted roles. And yet this sense that our roles are not primarily *defences* but open spaces – that our selves are to some extent given us in our encounters with others in these spaces – is grounded in a deep theological conviction, which does not depend on the capacities of concrete others. 'Who has the authority to tell the story of a life?' is, among others, a theological question. Religion is often associated with roles in both senses I have used: narrative and social. And it is true that religious faith and communities are a powerful source of roles, with all their potential and risks. Religious communities supply clearly defined social roles, which can be great goods if they offer frameworks by which to shape useful and meaningful lives; though it is also important to recognize that they can sometimes become lifeless or distorting. More importantly, perhaps, the Christian faith offers a very powerful narrative role: within its cosmic story of creation, fall, salvation, and sanctification, we are able to take our place as part of a larger narrative, in which we do not have to be perfect protagonists but can admit to failure and need for help.

In these ways, role-taking in both its social and narrative forms is essential to religious faith and can help to shape lives that display virtue and meaning. But even more than being about roles, faith and theology are precisely about their gaps: the times when our social roles break apart, whether by being overwhelmed or by being hollowed out;

and the times when our narrative roles – our sense of our life as a coherent story in which we play an integrative role – fail, whether because we realize that in cultivating our own story we have made other people unreal to ourselves and hurt them, or because our story appears to be coming to an abrupt end in the face of crisis or death. Psychology and philosophy have crucial things to say about such breaking points, including in therapeutic contexts. But theology says something quite different in kind to both of these.

Ultimately, theology suggests that we need roles because we are not yet ourselves. I do not mean this *primarily* in the obvious sense that selfhood within a role is always deferred: that a role is complete only when anagnorisis has been achieved (as by Othello, Lear, Leontes) and the poor player is finally dead (like Richard II, Macbeth, Hamlet, and Lear again); or when identity has been revealed (think of *As You Like It, Cymbeline, Pericles*) and the hapless hero is finally married (think of *Much Ado*). We are not, or not guaranteed to be, or never stably, in a play that moves towards such anagnorisis or catastrophe or reconciliation.

Rather, the claim that we need roles because we are not yet ourselves is rooted in the eschatological vision of the Psalmist, the writer of Job, and the New Testament writers. God's thoughts about us are precious and 'more numerous than the sand' – 'when I awake', the Psalmist marvels, 'I am still with thee'.[26] In other words, the deepest wellspring of who we are and how we are to orient ourselves in the world is found neither in fixed and impersonal values nor in the citadel of our inner selves, but in the calling and love of God. St Paul suggests that it is not in introspection but in allowing ourselves to be seen by God that we both are and know ourselves: 'For now we see through a glass, darkly; but then face to face: now I know in part; but then shall I know even as also I am known.'[27] For the New Testament writers (as, in a more limited sense, for Heidegger), this fullness of understanding is not achievable within earthly life, where all our actions are incomplete, and God remains partly hidden. It is an eschatological promise. C. S. Lewis asks provocatively at the end of his great late novel, 'How can the gods meet us face to face till we have faces?'.[28] But it is equally true to ask, 'How can we have faces until He meets us face to face?'.

I have already suggested the ways in which roles enable encounter. I will elaborate in the final chapter how it is such encounter, rather than roles in and of themselves, which most deeply anticipates eschatological personhood. For now, I conclude that on the one hand, we hope for a good role, unashamed, in the great play of history; on the other, we must remember how limited our seeing through roles is, how much we miss, how much we construct. We can only rely on the God who carries us. Our roles, like our images, are not towers to be defended, but boats in which to travel out to sea.

Notes

1. See Charles Guignon, *On Being Authentic* (London: Routledge, 2004). Histories and critiques related to Guignon's (and mine) are developed in Lionel Trilling, *Sincerity and Authenticity* (London: Oxford University Press, 1972); Charles Taylor, *The Ethics of Authenticity* (Cambridge, MA:

Harvard University Press, 1992). The ideal of authenticity is defended in sophisticated form e.g. in Jacob Golomb, *In Search of Authenticity: From Kierkegaard to Camus* (London: Routledge, 1995); Stanley Cavell, *In Quest of the Ordinary: Lines of Skepticism and Romanticism* (Chicago, IL: University of Chicago Press, 1988); Cavell, *Conditions Handsome and Unhandsome: The Constitution of Emersonian Perfectionism* (Chicago, IL: University of Chicago Press, 1990); Cavell, *Cities of Words: Pedagogical Letters on a Register of the Moral Life* (Cambridge, MA: Harvard University Press, 2004).

2. Charles Taylor, *A Secular Age* (Cambridge, MA: Harvard University Press, 2007), 27 and *passim*.

3. Stanley Cavell calls this attitude to others 'theatricalization': see a later section of this chapter, as well as Chapter 5.

4. See e.g. Søren Kierkegaard, *Attack upon 'Christendom,'* edited and translated by Walter Lowrie (Princeton, NJ: Princeton University Press, 1944); Heidegger, *Being and Time*, §27.

5. Kurt Vonnegut, *Mother Night* (New York: Avon, 1961), v.

6. See Charles Taylor, *Sources of the Self: The Making of the Modern Identity* (Cambridge, MA: Harvard University Press, 1989), 3–107.

7. See esp. Emmanuel Levinas, *Totalité et Infini: essai sur l'extériorité* (The Hague: Martinus Nijhoff, 1961), translated by Alphonso Lingis as *Totality and Infinity: An Essay on Exteriority* (Pittsburgh, PA: Duquesne University Press, 1969); Stanley Cavell, *The Claim of Reason: Wittgenstein, Skepticism, Morality, and Tragedy* (Oxford: Oxford University Press, 1979); Rowan Williams, *The Tragic Imagination* (Oxford: Oxford University Press, 2016). See also Terry Pinkard's excellent discussion of Sophocles' *Antigone*, and Hegel's use of it, in Pinkard, *Hegel's Phenomenology: The Sociality of Reason* (Cambridge: Cambridge University Press, 1994), 144–145.

8. For a complementary view of the contract-less-ness of romantic love itself, see Gillian Rose, *Love's Work* (New York: New York Review of Books, 1995), 60.
9. Katherine Hawley, *How to Be Trustworthy* (Oxford: Oxford University Press, 2020).
10. Samuel Beckett, *Endgame* (London: Faber, 1957), 33 and 41.
11. Cavell, 'The Avoidance of Love,' in *Must We Mean What We Say?*, 267–353, p. 333; reprinted in Cavell, *Disowning Knowledge: In Seven Plays of Shakespeare* (Cambridge: Cambridge University Press, 2012), 39–123, p. 104. See also the other chapters of Cavell, *Disowning Knowledge*.
12. Tzachi Zamir does sophisticated philosophical work in this space; see e.g. *Acts: Theater, Philosophy, and the Performing Self* (Ann Arbor, MI: University of Michigan Press, 2014).
13. Rowan Williams, *Being Human: Bodies, Minds, Persons* (Grand Rapids: Eerdmans, 2018), 11.
14. The same is, in a slightly different way, true of novels: It is the multiplicity of perspectives that makes a novel like George Eliot's *Middlemarch* (Edinburgh: William Blackwood, 1872) such a deep human experience.
15. William Shakespeare, *Pericles, Prince of Tyre*, edited by Doreen DelVecchio and Antony Hammond (Cambridge: Cambridge University Press, 1998), 21.182.
16. 'The Avoidance of Love,' in *Must We Mean What We Say?*, 333–334, and in *Disowning Knowledge*, 104. On the concept of the unavailability of the world, see esp. Stanley Rosen, *The Elusiveness of the Ordinary: Studies in the Possibility of Philosophy* (New Haven, CT: Yale University Press, 2002); Hartmut Rosa, *Unverfügbarkeit* (Berlin: Suhrkamp, 2018).
17. Samuel Beckett, *Play* (London: Faber, 1963), 64.
18. William Shakespeare, *The Winter's Tale*, edited by Stephen Orgel (Oxford: Oxford University Press, 1996), 3.2.53–56.

19. Shakespeare, *Winter's Tale*, 3.2.31–36.
20. Shakespeare, *Winter's Tale*, 3.2.79–80.
21. For a fuller reading of Beckett's late plays, see Erik Tonning, *Beckett's Abstract Drama* (Bern: Peter Lang, 2007).
22. Shakespeare, *Winter's Tale*, 5.3.94–95.
23. I give a fuller reading of *The Winter's Tale* in 'Hermione's Sophism: Ordinariness and Theatricality in *The Winter's Tale*,' *Philosophy and Literature* 39, no. 1A (2015), A83–105.
24. Chapter 5 will return to this theme.
25. Stanley Cavell, 'Knowing and Acknowledging,' in *Must We Mean What We Say?*, 238–266, p. 266.
26. Psalm 139.
27. 1 Corinthians 13.12.
28. C. S. Lewis, *Till We Have Faces* (London: Geoffrey Bles, 1956), pt 2, ch. 4.

3 | Bearing Ambiguity

It fills us to overflowing. We arrange it. It falls apart.
We rearrange it and fall apart ourselves.

Rilke, 'Eighth Duino Elegy'

Inheriting Roles, Inheriting Words

One of the contentions of the last chapter was that it is not possible conclusively to distinguish sincerity from pretence, either in ourselves or in others. Before any question of deceit, this is because in order to be intelligible, our actions must be performed and interpreted according to recognizable *patterns*, even if we improvise on those patterns. There is, as Wittgenstein has argued, no such thing as a private language because language – whether the language of gestures or of words – just *is* a network of signs and patterns that must be shared to function as what they are.[1] What we do and say is public not only in the sense of being communal, visible, subject to interpretation by others, but also in the sense of being *ahead* of any of us as individuals.[2] By assuming roles, by using language at all, we inhabit patterns that precede us; we are implicated in these patterns, step into their responsibilities, suffer their reverberations. We never *simply* act as individuals in the world: our gestures and words are inherited, and are therefore more than merely ours. We are, as Rowan Williams says, 'always defined by unchosen connections and the obligations that come with them'.[3]

Perhaps this burden of the inheritance of language is felt by no one more strongly than the poets of the twentieth century, after the cataclysms of the World Wars have made it seem hard, even morally dangerous, to step into the patterns of language and behaviour that structured a world that had come to this. T. S. Eliot's great poetic cycle *Four Quartets* is punctured by confrontations with this challenge of inheritance:

So here I am, in the middle way, having had twenty years—
Twenty years largely wasted, the years of *l'entre deux guerres*
Trying to use words, and every attempt
Is a wholly new start, and a different kind of failure
Because one has only learnt to get the better of words
For the thing one no longer has to say, or the way in which
One is no longer disposed to say it. And so each venture
Is a new beginning, a raid on the inarticulate
With shabby equipment always deteriorating
In the general mess of imprecision of feeling,
Undisciplined squads of emotion. And what there is
    to conquer
By strength and submission, has already been discovered
Once or twice, or several times, by men whom one
    cannot hope
To emulate—but there is no competition—
There is only the fight to recover what has been lost

And found and lost again and again: and now, under
   conditions
That seem unpropitious. But perhaps neither gain nor loss.
For us, there is only the trying. The rest is not our business.[4]

   The lines echo the exigencies of Chapter 2 here. Just as
there is very rarely a space that we share with others beyond
any roles, so there is very rarely a space beyond words: only
a 'general mess of imprecision of feeling / Undisciplined
squads of emotion' that do not amount to personhood. Yet
the fact that words are necessary is no guarantee that words
will suffice, nor does it absolve us of the responsibility of
inhabiting them.

   Sometimes there are crises so profound that such inhabitation becomes impossible, as it does for Leontes when the
meaning of his own words dissolves in the speaking, or for
Lear when all he can do is to speak the non-words, 'Howl,
howl, howl'.[5] There is no more striking example of this,
perhaps, than the poetry of Paul Celan, a German-speaking
Romanian Jew who translated Shakespeare's sonnets into
German while forced into hard labour in the Czernowitz
ghetto, whose parents were deported and perished in the
concentration camps, who volunteered for hard labour
in the later years of the war, who eventually emigrated to
Vienna and Paris, and who, after a stormy career as a poet,
committed suicide by drowning in the Seine.[6]

   Celan was confronted, as one who lived in language
and in the German language, by the corruption of that
language-world for the destruction of his people. To some
extent (as Hannah Arendt's reports on the Eichmann trial
made clear[7]), the Holocaust was a triumph of a language

unmoored from its responsibilities to an inchoate, living reality – a language forcing that reality into its own abstractions: 'extermination', 'Final Solution'. The phrase 'banality of evil' gestures to the insufferable superficiality of words unmoored from Eliot's 'general mess', and the great evil that it can be to force conformity to that shallowness.

Celan, therefore, finds himself having nothing but a language that is deeply corrupt. It is an act both of exigency and of profound courage that he does not simply abandon it, but dwells in that destitution. In Celan's poetry, language is tortured, broken, fragmented without any possibility of projecting the mirage of a word-world that is intact and meaningful. In his poetry, images from the great canons of religion and literature are mixed and fractured by experience, but also illuminate that experience in flashes, expanding it to something beyond itself. Celan's language *creates* without creating something *intact*. It is therefore vastly difficult poetry but, especially when encountered in crisis, also profoundly moving. Here is his 'Tenebrae':

> We are near, Lord,
> Near and seizable.
>
> Already seized, Lord,
> Tearing, torn into, as if
> The body of each of us were
> Your body, Lord.
>
> Pray, Lord,
> Pray to us,
> We are near.
> Wind-warped we went

We went to bow down
over swale and maar.

To the trough we went, Lord.

It was blood, it was
What you had spilt, Lord.

It glistened.

It cast your image into our eyes, Lord.
Eyes and mouth are so open and bare, Lord.
We have drunk, Lord.
The blood and the image in the blood, Lord.

Pray, Lord.
We are near.[8]

Neither Celan nor Eliot refuses the inheritance of language. Without inheritance, there is no imaginative creation and no possibility of healing. And yet our inherited world is never merely home.

Inhabiting Ambiguity

This chapter examines the condition, as Rilke puts it, of not being 'fully at home in our interpreted world'.[9] This condition arises in part from the dialectics of immersion and consciousness: the fact that we express ourselves in signs that we inherit and inhabit, and which do not accidentally but constitutively *abstract* from the 'general mess of imprecision' within. Even before any question of intention, the public nature of words and gestures makes it impossible conclusively to distinguish authenticity from pretence or delusion.

This gap between the abstraction of words and the imprecision of feeling or intention can be paralyzing when we find ourselves inhabiting roles we have outgrown or language that has lost traction. However, in more ordinary circumstances, this gap is not disruptive but, to the contrary, constitutive of our lives together. Social interaction is, for the most part, a continuous, incremental calibration of our words and actions to each other, mediated by ambiguity. Indeed, we are masters of ambiguity. We habitually offer words and actions which are not univocal, but compatible with a number of interpretations and which snap into a shared grid that is being tacitly and continuously negotiated.

This is especially marked in interactions that expose us to social risk: it is essential to flirtation that the approach should have plausible deniability; that it should be interpretable within the frameworks of attraction *and* of casual chatter. It is essential to some demands for action that they be interpretable as both casual approach and threat, or for certain threats to be interpretable as both jocular and serious. This constant deployment of ambiguity is the lubrication of day-to-day life. This also means, of course, that day-to-day life can pose immense challenges for conversation partners from different cultural and linguistic backgrounds, or for people with autism spectrum disorder, who find it difficult to decipher or live with such ambiguity.[10]

In other words, we always consciously or unconsciously inhabit gestures, words, and roles. To do so – both to act and to interpret action – requires imaginative integration: stretching underdetermined acts or trimming overdetermined ones to fit a framework within which they make sense. The resulting gestalt is never exactly the same for all conversation partners, because the gap between 'mess of imprecision' and sense-making pattern is ineliminable, and because people's sense-making patterns are never identical. (This is partly why it is a feeling of such profound joy and comfort when we find someone who sees things just as we see them. 'What? You too? I thought I was the only one.'[11]) Without ambiguity, we could not live together, and to demand a language that eliminates ambiguity is to seek to abolish language. But this condition also implies that living together is always laden with responsibility. As suggested in the last chapter, a certain virtuosity is possible, even needed, in inhabiting the world: To act and speak with virtue and virtuosity means, among other things, to open up possibilities for others by the ways in which we interpret their behaviour to them and give them space to develop.

However, such attentiveness has to be learnt. For the most part, as noted in Chapter 1, our own imaginative activity is hidden from us: it functions habitually and unconsciously, without awareness of its own agency. The words on a page seem self-evidently to mean one thing; people appear self-evidently rude or haughty. In seeming merely to find what in fact we also construe, we are immersed in patterns and impressions that appear fixed and incontrovertible, while in fact being highly malleable. Poets, through their strange ways of attending to, testing, and rearranging words and verbal patterns, make visible the gaps within and beneath language, and make possible new ways of seeing.

This is not a frivolous exercise, but in its own way is as important as therapy: it brings to consciousness the work of inhabiting our interpreted world, and exercises the skills to perform it. And unlike some forms of therapy, poetry does not do so by trying to eliminate the risk of deception, delusion, and error, because this would be a false security. We are human; there's no cure for that.[12] Rather, poets like Rilke, Eliot, or Celan tell us that such risk is intrinsic to our lives on earth, where we are never fully or merely at home; and they give us the courage to bear and engage it creatively.

I take such perceptual courage to be a characteristic virtue not only of poetry but of art – visual, literary, and musical – more generally. Eliciting the beholder's imaginative power is not a by-product of artistic creation, but one of its core aims. By reducing data points, by withholding context, and by juxtaposing incongruent material, artists invite their viewers and readers to construct new or unusual wholes: to see a three-dimensional space in two-dimensional lines or dots (Fig. 13), to see love in a rose, or the Blessed Virgin in an old charwoman (Fig. 14).[13] These new wholes offer second lenses, descants, or echoes of or over the ordinary world: Rather than forcing it into a different pattern, they enable an imaginative 'double' or 'depth' vision of the world.[14] As Merleau-Ponty puts it, 'Rather than seeing [the painting], I see according to, or with it.'[15]

The next three sections of this chapter offer a closer examination of these dynamics. To concretize my claims, I will turn first to visual perception and visual art, taking up certain claims of Chapter 1 and relating them to contemporary psychological theories of perception. I

Fig. 13 Maximillien Luce, *Morning, Interior*, 1890. Oil on canvas, 64.8 × 81.0 cm; The Metropolitan Museum of Fine Art, New York, United States of America. Bequest of Miss Adelaide Milton de Groot (1876–1967), 1967.

will then apply the principles formulated to the poetic art with which the chapter opened. In the final section, I will prepare the work of the following two chapters by beginning to show the relevance of these experiences with art to an understanding of the religious imagination. At the end of the chapter, and more fully in those following, I will discuss religious faith as at once caught up in the universal dynamic of finding and making and capable of anchoring that dynamic in a form of existential apophasis.

Fig. 14 Paul Cezanne, *An Old Woman with a Rosary*, 1895–1896. Oil on canvas, 80.6 × 65.5 cm; The National Gallery, London, UK.

Imagination as Gestalt Formation

The dynamics of art perception are a special case of the more general dynamics of image perception. Chapter 1 of this book introduced image perception by discussing the interaction between 'bottom-up'-sense impressions and 'top-down' patterns or expectations. Predictive processing is one contemporary theory concretizing these claims. The core claim of predictive processing (or predictive coding) is that one of the brain's primary functions, below the level of conscious interpretation, is to generate predictions about what it will perceive or do. Perception is not a one-way stream of impressions informing the mind, but rather a two-way stream: a bottom-up stream of sensory data and a top-down stream of predictions. The bottom-up stream starts with all the sense impressions we need to process. The top-down stream starts with all our accumulated predictions (or 'priors') about the world: our basic concepts and convictions, everything we know from previous experience, our familiarity with a specific context, and so forth. These priors predict what it is that we are seeing, and perception takes the form of checking to what extent the sensory input conforms to those predictions.

If sensory input and prediction do not accord, the brain (still below the level of conscious or personal decision) registers a prediction error, which needs to be resolved. And this can happen in two ways: either by adjusting what sense impressions are channelled upwards or by adjusting the patterns into which we organize them. Which of these we do depends on our relative confidence, within a specific context, in our sense impressions versus our predictions: whether the day is foggy or clear, for example, or whether we think we know what's in front of us or find an unknown object that could be anything.

Our priors or expectations, according to this theory, are ordered in a hierarchical cascade: the low-level or specific prediction that a small flying shape I encounter in a forest is more likely to be a butterfly than a fairy is informed by higher-level or more general predictions about the population of Scottish forests, and yet more general predictions about the constitution of the world. Conflicts between sense data and predictions that cannot be resolved at a low level (e.g. by adjusting the way one sees or slightly adjusting one's expectations) 'travel up' to be resolved at a higher level – and sometimes, they may be strong enough to require us to adjust high-level predictions about the world, as happens in a powerful conversion experience.

This dynamic (whether expressed in terms of predictive processing or not) is evident in visual illusions like the duck–rabbit (Fig. 15) and Necker's cube (Fig. 1), which

Fig. 15 Anonymous, *Rabbit and Duck*, 1882. Etching. In *Fliegende Blätter*, 23 October 1882.

bring the work of perception to consciousness by stripping the drawings of the kind of disambiguating context that usually helps us resolve what we are seeing. Wittgenstein famously observed that in looking at Fig. 15, we do not first see a set of lines which we then consciously overlay with an interpretation of their sense; rather, such sense-making is instantaneous: we always see the lines *as* something, even if that something is not stable but liable to give way to something else.[16] This constructive moment within perception itself is usually masked by a clarifying context that makes it more or less matter-of-course. In this case, however, that context is removed and the active moment of interpretation exposed.

In illusions such as the rotating mask[17] and the Ames Room (see Fig. 9), the converse is foregrounded. Rather than sense data being precise and the conditions for specific predictions suppressed, the illusions elicit strong predictions to which our sense impressions conform.[18] For most neurotypical viewers, the rotating mask will switch aspects and seem to face forward (rather than backward, as it actually does) about two-thirds through its rotation.[19] Similarly, the Ames Room will appear as an ordinarily shaped room. In fact, of course, the room extends backward on one side, and what look like regular floor patterns and equally sized doors are in fact highly unusual trapezoidal shapes. The illusion arises from the conviction that there can only be one way of interpreting the visual pattern in front of us. We are, as Ernst Gombrich puts it, 'blind to the other possible configurations because we literally "cannot imagine" these unlikely objects. They have no name and no habitation in the universe of our experience'.[20]

This kind of active pattern-matching, usually guided 'blindly' (in Kant's sense) by expectations which are built up through context and previous experience, goes on all the time in ordinary life, but we are rarely aware of it. It springs into consciousness on occasion, such as when we jump, startled, at the sight of a bug, only to realize that it is in fact a leaf (Fig. 16); or when we have read an email or text message as saying what we expected, and only later find that we have misread it. Object identification by means of learnt pattern-matching is, of course, a dominant mode of AI learning, used in the face-recognition tools of photo libraries and social media or in the autocorrect function of messaging services. There are great variations in the ways people correlate expectation and sensory attention, some located on a spectrum of personality differences (such as certain aspects of 'openness' in the Big Five personality model), others on a spectrum of sensory processing patterns (such as pareidolia, the heightened tendency to see faces in clouds, curtains, or other shapes, as in Fig. 5). The insistence on imposing meaningful patterns on random sense perception can take extreme forms in schizophrenia, which is in part a debilitating compulsion to see intentional patterns where there are none. But even under ordinary conditions, we tend to rely increasingly on expected patterns or priors as we age, maybe because they have accumulated such weight compared to sensory input; which is why it is very important to exercise the imagination.

Fig. 16 Bernard Dupont, *Giant Leaf Insect (Phyllium giganteum)*, 2013. Photograph; Butterfly Farm, Pahang, Malaysia. Credit: Bernard Dupont, CC BY-SA 2.0 Deed.

Art and Illusion

The ability to pattern-match, which goes on in everyday life, also underlies our ability to understand visual art, in which sensory data is always incomplete. Sometimes, artists merely exploit this ability, especially in creating optical illusions such as trompe l'œil or forced perspectives. More typically, however, artists deliberately prescind from making their illusions complete. This is because, as the art historian Ernst Gombrich observes,

> [o]ur pleasure in illusion ... rests precisely in the mind's effort in bridging the difference between art and reality. This very pleasure is destroyed when the illusion is too complete. 'When the painter packs a vast expanse into a narrow space, when he leads me across the depths of the infinite on a flat surface, and makes the air circulate .... I love to abandon myself to his illusions, but I want the frame to be there, I want to know that what I see is actually nothing but a canvas or a simple plane.'[21]

In Michael Polanyi's words, 'The factual information content of art is slight, its main purpose being to evoke our participation in its utterance.'[22]

The history of modern painting can, in part, be told as a history of the changing directions of this purpose. Impressionism (flourishing in the second half of the nineteenth century) strove to capture the visual experience of a scene in all its dynamism and ephemerality by enlisting the beholder's participation in the act of seeing. By eschewing familiar schematisms, impressionist paintings remind us that if we did not already *know* that these were horses (Fig. 17) and these lilies (Fig. 2), we would not *see* them as such. The remarkable vitality of these paintings comes from a creative collaboration between the artist's detailed observation and the beholder's imagination: the living

Fig. 17 Édouard Manet, *At the Races*, 1875. Oil on panel, 38.7 × 51.1 cm; Widener Collection, National Gallery of Art, Washington, DC, USA.

dynamism of our imaginative impression of a gestalt on a riot of colours.

Expressionism (flourishing in the first half of the twentieth century) radicalized this dynamic. Where impressionism still aimed for a collaboration between unstructured sense impression and gestalt or schema, expressionism deliberately set the two at odds with each other. The elements of an expressionist painting resist being integrated straightforwardly into a form or whole such as we might encounter in the real world. They gesture in that direction but do not allow the beholder to complete the gesture. Where in space is Kokoschka's *Still Life with Mutton and Hyacinth* (1910) arranged (Fig. 18)? How do the elements of Picasso's *Still Life* (1918)

Fig. 18 Oskar Kokoschka, *Still Life with Mutton and Hyacinth,*
1910. Multimedia, 37.6 × 27.4 cm; Österreichische Galerie
Belvedere, Vienna, Austria. Credit: © Fondation Oskar Kokoschka
/ DACS 2023. Photo: Belvedere, Vienna.

relate to themselves, each other, and space (Fig. 19)?
These paintings bring to consciousness the perpetual
(and usually unconscious) endeavour to read or see elements according to a whole, precisely by frustrating that
endeavour. Sometimes, as in Picasso's *Weeping Woman*
(1937), incoherence on the sensory level can be resolved
into sense on a semantic or figurative level: This woman
appears broken because she is broken on the inside; her
pictorial disjointedness is not incidental but precisely
expressionistic (Fig. 20). Similarly, Salvador Dalí's phan-
tasmagorical shapes are expressive of the sometimes

Fig. 19 Pablo Picasso, *Still Life*, 1918. Oil on canvas, 97.2 × 130.2 cm; Chester Dale Collection, National Gallery of Art, Washington, DC, USA. Credit: © Succession Picasso / DACS, London 2023. Photo: National Gallery of Art.

threatening uncanniness of the world encountered by the senses (Fig. 21).

Modern and postmodern art (flourishing in the second half of the twentieth century) explored endless variations of this ability to create a conflict between immediate sensory data and imaginatively projected gestalt, aimed not at a single effect but at a deliberate multiplicity of responses. Readymades (such as Fig. 22) remove everyday objects from the contexts within which they ordinarily make sense, and create a jarring interpretative context through titling and spatial positioning. Indeterminate art

Fig. 20 Pablo Picasso, *Weeping Woman*, 1937. Oil on canvas, 60.8 × 50.0 cm; Tate, London, UK. Credit: © Succession Picasso / DACS, London 2023. Photo: Tate.

(such as Fig. 23) and abstract art (such as Fig. 8) stimulate the beholder's attempt to see form or meaning, only to frustrate that attempt on the pictorial level. The effect of this interruption of the interpretative process is purposely

Fig. 21 Salvador Dalí, *The Temptation of St. Anthony*, 1946. Oil on canvas, 90.0 cm × 119.5 cm; Musées Royaux des Beaux-Arts de Belgique, Brussels, Belgium. Credit: © Salvador Dali, Fundació Gala-Salvador Dalí, DACS 2023. Photo: © Fine Art Images / Bridgeman Images.

left to the viewer: some feel excited at a seeming endless-ness of possibilities; some are frustrated by the thwarting of an aim-directed faculty; some feel bored because there is no sense to be found; some are moved to reflect on the processes the encounter triggers in them; some relax because no goal-directedness is here necessary; others have any number of other responses. In all these cases, the anxiety of interpretation common to all art interpretation ('Am I just making this interpretation up?') is not neutral-ized but deliberately sustained.

Fig. 22 Marcel Duchamp, *Bicycle Wheel*, 1963. Mixed media, 130 × 64 × 42 cm; private collection. Credit: © Association Marcel Duchamp / ADAGP, Paris and DACS, London 2024. Photo: Cameraphoto Arte Venezia / Bridgeman Images.

Fig. 23 Robert Pepperell, *Succulus*, 2005. Oil on panel, 123 × 123 cm. Credit: Robert Pepperell. Photo: Robert Pepperell.

Metaphor as Depth Perception

These visual conditions echo the verbal conditions discussed at the beginning of this chapter. The poetic tradition has its own versions of the experiments in visual art that I have recounted. In this section, however, I want not to re-narrate the history of poetry's evocation of our participation in its utterance, but to attend to one of its basic forms. Like visual art, poetry elicits and plays with our capacity to lend form to data that is disparate, incongruous, or incomplete.[23] This aesthetic play is not frivolous but in some sense necessary, because the world as we encounter it always, in a sense, needs it. Rowan Williams says about the poet that '[t]he reality before him is obscurely incomplete: it proposes to the poet the task of making it significant – which does not mean imposing upon it an alien structure of explanation'.[24] Similarly, Jacques Maritain sees poetry as the 'recomposition' of 'a world more real than the reality offered to the senses'.[25]

These dynamics are at work at all levels of poetry, especially its simplest and most essential form, namely figurative language. Consider this small handful of metaphors in poetry:

> Soundlessly they go,
> the herons passing by:
> arrows of snow
> filling the sky.
>
> Yamazaki Sōkan (1464–1552)

> Shall I compare thee to a summer's day?
>
> William Shakespeare (1564–1616), 'Sonnet 18'

> Like a heavy fragrance
> snowflakes settle:
> lilies on rocks.
>
> Matsuo Basho (1644–1694)

> The apparition of these faces in the crowd:
> Petals on a wet, black bough.
>
> Ezra Pound (1885–1972), 'In a Station of the Metro'

And how dismayed is any womb-born thing
that has to fly! As though it were afraid
of its own self, it zigzags through the air
like crack through cup. Thus the track of a bat
rends through the evening's porcelain.
> Rainer Maria Rilke (1875–1926), 'Eighth Duino Elegy'

The cold smell of potato mould, the squelch and slap
Of soggy peat, the curt cuts of an edge
Through living roots awaken in my head.
But I've no spade to follow men like them.

Between my finger and my thumb
The squat pen rests.
I'll dig with it.
> Seamus Heaney (1939–2013), 'Digging'[26]

Each of these images rouses their readers' imagination to see in ways that at once attenuate and intensify ordinary perception. They hold before our mental eye two distinct realities or objects and invite us, by the exercise of our integrative power of perception, to see them *together*, to see one through and in the other: to see, as through a stereoscope, a double or depth vision in the conjunction of digging and writing; of the zigzag of a bat's flight and a crack in porcelain; of faces and petals; snow and lilies; herons and arrows. This brings our own imagination to consciousness precisely as a search for meaning that is to be found not only in the poetic text, but in the world at large. For the search is, in a sense, for a *depth* of world at which these different things are related. Just as we project a space within which the lines on a canvas make sense, so we project a space in which these two images can be held in one vision.[27]

None of these projections comes with any truth claims. Neither poet nor reader claims that writing and digging are, in fact, the same. Rather, what truth they have depends on the acts of seeing, thinking, and acting that they make possible. Metaphors are, in Heidegger's sense, formal indications: not truths to be learned but paths to be walked.[28] This is why the risk of over-interpreting poetry is ineradicable (we can never know whether a certain meaning is 'really there'), but not deleterious, because the responsibility rests, in any case, with us. The question is not so much what meanings are unambiguously present, but what possibilities are opened and closed by certain ways of seeing. Adjudicating and making use of these possibilities is the responsibility of the reader. This is also why good literary criticism can be a participation in the work of a poem or text: it can be an extension of its imaginative reach, and an interrogation of its presuppositions, limits, chances, and dangers.

Yet, as I have just suggested, the imaginative engagement of metaphors is not merely playful or wholly subjective. The possibility and pleasure of such metaphorical 'seeing-as' depend on a deep innate desire to connect things: to trace patterns through different layers and domains of existence. Aristotle observed that 'to metaphorize well implies an intuitive perception of the similarity in dissimilars'.[29] This is not a marginal human ability but a central one. As I have said, *all* perception to some extent depends on it: we must be capable of seeing similarities or patterns in vastly disparate sense impressions to recognize objects at all. The capacity to see metaphors – to imagine one thing in and as another, and to imagine the world as connected in this way – foregrounds the remarkable intertwining of finding and making in this ordinary human capacity. As Paul Ricœur put it, 'metaphor "invents" in both senses of the word: what it creates, it discovers; and what it finds, it invents'.[30]

Ricœur himself derives a striking claim from this dynamic:

> My deepest conviction is that poetic language alone restores to us that participation-in or belonging-to an order of things which precedes our capacity to oppose ourselves to things taken as objects opposed to a subject. Hence the function of poetic discourse is to bring about this emergence of a depth-structure of belonging-to amid the ruins of descriptive discourse.[31]

For Ricœur, in other words, the human ability to create and understand metaphors reveals a profound truth not only about our cognitive apparatus, but about the world in which such breadth and depth of connections are to be found – just as the ability to create scientific models and mathematical formulae reveals a profound truth about the deep *knowability* and therefore potential meaningfulness of the world. In order to see metaphors, there must be a depth-structure in which they make sense.

Faith and Perceptual Renewal: Liturgy and Scripture

The suggestion that our imaginative capacity may, in some sense, be adequate to the world beyond it, or reveal something about its structure, opens a theological horizon to the theme of this chapter. Indeed, the Christian faith has at its heart a belief that the human capacity and need to imagine is in significant ways fitting (or, in the old Scholastic sense, 'convenient') to the nature of reality: that the world is poetic, both in the sense that it is the work or *poema* of God and in the sense that it is realized through co-creation. The two are not in competition: as many spiritual writers have observed, time and love are genuinely there to be found, but they cannot be found without being made. Christian faith therefore manifests itself, among other things, as a mode of seeing the ordinary world which invests that world imaginatively (or inspiredly) with an unseen depth of divine intention and spiritual significance. It brings to things in general some of the attitudes that people ordinarily bring to works of art: an expectation that there is something here to be found, and a willingness to participate in its utterance.[32]

This is why metaphor is at the very heart of the Christian imagination. The painter David Jones said that it would be unthinkable 'that at the Redemption of the World anything should have been done which committed man to any activity not utterly inalienable from his nature. In such a context the extraneous is inconceivable'.[33] The Lord's choice, on the night before he was betrayed, to take bread and wine and declare them his body and blood was not an artificial illustration of his work of redemption or a mechanical mechanism for its transmission; rather, it named and transformed a mystery that lies near the heart of human existence. The Last Supper made into fact what can usually exist only as poetic invention.[34] In identifying bread and wine with body and blood, it is what we might call a 'literal metaphor', carrying something over from one form of reality to another: It is an instance of 'seeing-as' which, in imagining, truly finds.

This 'carrying over' or *metaphora* remains a continual task of faith and theology. Much of the Christian faith is centred on metaphors whose truth is both found and made, real beyond our imagining and yet ours to make. 'The Body of Christ' is perhaps the most striking example of this: while in some sense already localized in the Eucharist (and, after an earthly sojourn, at the Father's right hand), it is also a designation of the Church, whose shape will not be known fully until the eschaton. This body is itself constituted through the Eucharistic liturgy, and the dynamic interrelation between the Eucharist and the Church as 'the Body of Christ' reveals a complexity, seriousness, and depth of imaginative exchange that exceeds any engagement with art.

The Eucharistic liturgy understands itself as a living image of the eschatological wedding feast of the Lamb, in which worshippers are enabled to participate proleptically in body, spirit, and imagination.[35] This spiritual participation is not merely anticipatory but also formative: it helps to transform worshippers into the body and the bride who will one day sit at the wedding feast of the new creation. This alchemy requires that worshippers identify with the broken body of Jesus in a way that is not arrogation but confession: to confess that they are internally broken and need both to receive and to be taken into Christ's body. This is what happens at the Eucharist; as Martin Luther puts it, 'when the body eats it physically, this food digests the body's flesh and transforms it so that it too becomes spiritual'.[36] Yet it is equally significant to this existential exchange that the Mass takes its name not from its consummation but from its dissolution: *Ite, missa est* – 'Go, a sending has taken place'. To grow into the body of Christ, worshippers cannot remain at the liturgy, but must go out 'and do likewise'; they must return to their ordinary lives in the light of this event. In the final chapter, we will return to this dispersion in more depth.

More immediately related to ordinary artistic forms than the liturgy is the Bible, which is now habitually taught as literature.[37] Paul Ricœur calls the Bible a poem, and this is true among other ways in the sense that the Bible elicits imaginative participation. As in the liturgy, this participation is more existential and serious than in an ordinary poem: the Bible's images are (for those who believe in it) uniquely load-bearing; inviting readers to pour themselves into them unreservedly, though never without risk. As Rowan Williams puts it, 'Revelation, on such an account, is essentially to do with what is *generative* in our experience – events or transactions in our language that break existing frames of reference and initiate new possibilities of life.'[38]

Consequently, one of the primary ways the biblical narratives inspire and teach is by engendering perceptual shifts – shifts from perceiving one 'whole' or 'form' in one's world to perceiving another. This is the case both for characters within these stories and for their readers. Many biblical stories turn on their characters' sudden ability to see their world or lives no longer as one thing but as another – to perceive them as forming a gestalt they did not previously see. This is especially striking in the prophetic and wisdom literature. In the Book of Jonah, God raises up a gourd tree so that his prophet may learn to see the Ninevites anew, as people 'who cannot tell their right hand from their left', eliciting God's concern as the gourd tree elicits Jonah's. More expansively, in the Book of Job, Job ultimately does not find explanations but experiences a radical perspectival shift: in God's self-manifestation, his perception of the shape of the world and his own place in it change. In the Gospel, Jesus encourages Martha to see the world afresh when he urges that Mary has chosen the better part. After his resurrection, he enables Mary of Magdala, Thomas Didymus, the disciples on the road to Emmaus, and his persecutor Saul to see him – and with him the entire story of which they are part – anew. These conversions comprise not so much deliberate decisions as sudden shifts of perspective. His disciples come to *see* Jesus as 'my Lord and my God' (John 20.28). To see him thus transforms their vision not only of him, but with him also of the world, themselves, and how they are to speak, act, and live.[39]

Biblical stories not only recount experiences of gestalt shifts, but as importantly aim to inspire such shifts in their readers. John's Gospel immediately commends Thomas's realization to his readers: 'Blessed are those who do not see and yet believe.' Many of the Scriptures' parables likewise aim to inspire new ways of seeing ordinary circumstances: thus, 1 Corinthians 12 trains its readers to see the people of Christ as a body conjoined, and Matthew 25, likewise, to see the stranger and the prisoner as, in some sense, Christ (Fig. 24). The mental transformations engendered here are aptly described by the Greek *metanoia*, 'conversion' or

Fig. 24 Timothy P. Schmalz, *Homeless Jesus*, 2013. Sculpture in bronze, 91 × 61 × 213 cm; Metropolitan Cathedral, Buenos Aires, Argentina. Credit: 'Homeless Jesus' by sculptor Timothy P. Schmalz – sculpturebytps.com. Photo: Dennis Jarvis.

'renewal of the mind'. And like *metanoia*, they imply not only a passive change of perception, or even an active reimagination, but also the responsibility to enact these in life, without any ultimate guarantees.

Notes

1. Wittgenstein, *Philosophical Investigations*, pt 1, §§243–315. There is a voluminous literature on Wittgenstein's arguments against the possibility of a private language. The classic touchpoint is Saul Kripke, *Wittgenstein on Rules and Private Language* (Oxford: Blackwell, 1982); see esp. also Stephen

Mulhall, *Wittgenstein's Private Language: Grammar, Nonsense, and Imagination in Philosophical Investigations*, *243–315* (Oxford: Oxford University Press, 2007).

2. See esp. Stephen Mulhall's interpretation of Heidegger's 'They' ('*das Man*') in the *Routledge Guidebook to Heidegger's Being and Time* (London: Routledge, 2nd ed., 2013), ch. 2. See also Charles Taylor, *The Language Animal* (Cambridge, MA: Harvard University Press, 2016).

3. Rowan Williams, *The Edge of Words: God and the Habits of Language* (London: Bloomsbury, 2014), 13.

4. T. S. Eliot, 'East Coker,' in *Four Quartets* (London: Faber, 1941), V.

5. William Shakespeare, *The Tragedy of King Lear*, edited by Jay L. Halio (Cambridge: Cambridge University Press, 1992), 5.3.256.

6. See John Felstiner, *Paul Celan: Poet, Survivor, Jew* (New Haven, CT: Yale University Press, 2001).

7. Hannah Arendt, *Eichmann in Jerusalem, or: The Banality of Evil* (New York: Viking Press, 1963).

8. Paul Celan, 'Tenebrae,' in *Sprachgitter* (Frankfurt: S. Fischer Verlag, 1957) (translation mine).

9. Rainer Maria Rilke, 'Erste Elegie,' in *Duineser Elegien* (Leipzig: Insel-Verlag, 1923), translated by Stephen Mitchell as *The Duino Elegies* in *The Selected Poetry of Rainer Maria Rilke* (New York: Random House, 1980), 150.

10. For a review of evidence relating autism to differences in predictive processing, see Jonathan Cannon, Amanda M. O'Brien, Lindsey Bungert, and Pawan Sinha, 'Prediction in Autism Spectrum Disorder: A Systematic Review of Empirical Evidence,' *Autism Research* 14, no. 4 (2021), 604–630.

11. See C. S. Lewis, *The Four Loves* (London: Geoffrey Bles, 1960), ch. 4.

12. This is the consistent tenor of Cavell's early work; see esp. 'Knowing and Acknowledging' and *The Claim of Reason*.

13. For a reading of Cezanne's *An Old Woman with a Rosary*, see Judith Wolfe, 'Imagining God,' *Modern Theology* 40, no. 1 (2024), 97–109, p. 109.

14. My use of this term is borrowed from Tzachi Zamir, *Double Vision: Moral Philosophy and Shakespearean Drama* (Princeton, NJ: Princeton University Press, 2006).

15. Maurice Merleau-Ponty, 'Eye and Mind,' in *The Merleau-Ponty Aesthetics Reader: Philosophy and Painting*, edited by Galen A. Johnson (Evanston, IL: Northwestern University Press, 1993), 121–150, p. 126.

16. Wittgenstein, *Philosophical Investigations*, pt 2, §xi.

17. See e.g. eChalk, 'The Rotating Mask Illusion,' YouTube, 20 July 2012, www.youtube.com/watch?v=sKaoeaKsdAo (accessed 17 January 2024).

18. Another well-known example is Christopher Chabris's and Daniel Simons's selective attention test, 'The Invisible Gorilla' (1999); see www.theinvisiblegorilla.com and www.youtube.com/watch?v=vJG698U2Mvo (accessed 17 January 2024).

19. Some neurodivergences correlate with immunity to the rotating mask illusion; see e.g. Danai Dima, Jonathan P. Roiser, Detlef E. Dietrich, Catharina Bonnemann, Heinrich Lanfermann, Hinderk M. Emrich, and Wolfgang Dillo, 'Understanding Why Patients with Schizophrenia Do Not Perceive the Hollow-Mask Illusion Using Dynamic Causal Modelling,' *NeuroImage* 46, no. 4 (2009), 1180–1186.

20. Gombrich, *Art and Illusion*, 200.

21. Gombrich, *Art and Illusion*, 224.

22. Michael Polanyi, 'What Is a Painting?,' *British Journal of Aesthetics* 10, no. 3 (1970): 225–236, p. 232.

23. Experimental studies show that people are readier to do this when they take a sentence to be poetry than when they take the same sentence to be ordinary prose; see Marina Iosifyan and Judith Wolfe, 'Poetry vs Everyday Life: Context Increases Perceived Meaningfulness of Sentences' (under review).
24. Rowan Williams, 'Poetic and Religious Imagination,' *Theology* 80, no. 675 (1977), 179–180.
25. Jacques Maritain, 'The Frontiers of Poetry,' in *Art and Scholasticism with Other Essays*, translated by James F. Scanlan (London: Sheed & Ward, 1946), 75.
26. Yamazaki Sōkan and Matsuo Basho as rendered by Michael R. Burch at: https://allpoetry.com/poem/14916123-Ancient-Haiku-by-Michael-R.-Burch (accessed 20 January 2024); William Shakespeare, 'Sonnet 18,' in *Shakespeare's Sonnets*, edited by Katherine Duncan-Jones (London: Bloomsbury, 2nd ed., 2010), 147; Ezra Pound, 'In a Station of the Metro,' *Poetry: A Magazine of Verse* (1913); Rainer Maria Rilke, 'Eighth Elegy,' in *Duino Elegies*; Seamus Heaney, 'Digging,' in *Death of a Naturalist* (London: Faber, 1966).
27. The literature on metaphor is vast. See esp. Nelson Goodman, *Languages of Art* (Indianapolis, IN: Hackett Publishing Company, 1976); Janet Soskice, *Metaphor and Religious Language* (Oxford: Clarendon Press, 1985); Paul Ricœur, *The Rule of Metaphor: The Creation of Meaning in Language* (London: Routledge, 1986); George Lakoff and Mark Johnson, *Metaphors We Live By* (Chicago, IL: University of Chicago Press, 1980); Gilles Fauconnier and Mark Turner, *The Way We Think: Conceptual Blending and the Mind's Hidden Complexities* (New York: Basic Books, 2002); Ted Cohen, *Thinking of Others: On the Talent for Metaphor* (Princeton, NJ: Princeton University Press, 2012); Denis Donoghue, *Metaphor* (Cambridge, MA: Harvard University

Press, 2014); Keith Holyoak, *The Spider's Thread: Metaphor in Mind, Brain, and Poetry* (Boston, MA: MIT Press, 2019)

28. See Heidegger, *Being and Time*, §25. A good English-language discussion of this section is Ryan Streeter, 'Heidegger's Formal Indication: A Question of Method in *Being and Time*,' *Man and World* 30 (1997), 413–430, p. 413.

29. Aristotle, *Poetics* 1459ª5–8, cited in Ricœur, *The Rule of Metaphor*, 6.

30. Ricœur, *The Rule of Metaphor*, 239.

31. Paul Ricœur, *Essays on Biblical Interpretation* (London: SPCK, 1981), 101.

32. As noted in Chapter 1, although I will later move into specifically Christian doctrine, it is beyond the aims of this book to offer any direct comparison of Christian thought with that of other religions; this should be done in concrete dialogue with practitioners of other faiths.

33. David Jones, 'Art and Sacrament,' in *Epoch and Artist* (London: Faber, 1959).

34. For similar arguments concerning the Incarnation, see C. S. Lewis, 'Myth Became Fact,' in *God in the Dock* (London: Fontana, 1979), 54–60; Austin Farrer, *The Glass of Vision* (Glasgow: Glasgow University Press, 1948).

35. See e.g. the *Catechism of the Catholic Church* (London: Catholic Truth Society, 1994), 259. Catherine Pickstock gives a seminal account of such participation in *After Writing: On the Liturgical Consummation of Philosophy* (Oxford: Blackwell, 1998).

36. Martin Luther, 'A Beautiful Sermon on the Reception of the Holy Sacrament,' in *Luther's Works*, edited by Jaroslav Pelikan (St Louis, MO: Concordia Publishing House, 1955–86), 37:100–101.

37. But see the criticisms of this framing by T. S. Eliot, 'Religion and Literature,' in *Faith that Illuminates*, edited by Vigo A. Demant (London: Centenary Press, 1935), 29–54; and C. S. Lewis, 'The Literary Impact of the Authorised Version' (London: Athlone Press, 1950).

38. Rowan Williams, 'Trinity and Revelation,' *Modern Theology* 2, no. 3 (1986), 197–212, p. 199. See also T. S. Eliot, 'Religion and Literature,' in *The Complete Prose of T.S. Eliot, Volume 5: Tradition and Orthodoxy, 1934–1939*, edited by Iman Javadi, Ronald Schuchard, and Jayme Stayer (Baltimore, MD: Johns Hopkins University Press, 2017), 218–229.

39. For a relevant reading of the resurrection narratives, see Brian D. Robinette, *Grammars of Resurrection: A Christian Theology of Presence and Absence* (New York: Crossroad / Herder & Herder, 2009).

4 | Looking for God

Look, I live. From what?
… Superabundant being
wells up in my heart.

Rilke, 'Ninth Duino Elegy'

In the course of the last chapter, I argued that visual images emerge from the imaginative organization of two-dimensional lines within a projected three-dimensional space. In ordinary representational art, this projection is rendered relatively unambiguous by two factors: the visual context of a scene and our own past experience. But sometimes, the projection of space is rendered ambiguous because one of these factors is withheld. In the case of the duck–rabbit or Necker's cube, what is withheld is pictorial context: we are unable to arbitrate between different aspects, different ways of seeing the figure, because the organizing space is implied only by the lines themselves. There is nothing that counts as relevant context, and so it is primarily our own prior experience that guides our interpretation. But in the case of the Ames Room or the rotating mask illusion, such prior experience confounds rather than confirms the data in front of us: we have seen so many convex faces and so few concave ones that we have immense trouble seeing the mask as concave or the room as trapezoidal.

For all the psychological interest of these illusions, the difficulties they create do not seem to infect our wider lives, because we have enough experience with rabbits, ducks, faces, and three-dimensional space to disambiguate our seeing. However, they make visible the amount of pattern-matching that goes into all seeing, and which is operative also in the more complex forms of 'seeing' which I have described as seeing a person, seeing a life, and seeing a world. In Chapter 2, I discussed the difficulty of matching to the patterns of roles an inner life which is not readily accessible (to us or others) independently of these roles, and in Chapter 3, I discussed the necessity and risks of casting in the patterns of language what is a 'general mess of imprecision of feeling' without language, yet can never be fully captured in it. Above all, in Chapter 1 and again at the end of Chapter 3, I talked about imaginative seeing at the most inclusive level: matching the varied and shifting impressions that make up our life in the world to the patterns of overarching frameworks which give them organization and meaning.

Unlike in the case of simple seeing, where we are able continuously to compare data with patterns and our seeing with that of others, and only rarely leave well-trodden paths of perception, there are no such safeguards in the case of our 'seeing' of other people and of reality at large. Neither in relation to people nor to the world as a whole do we have independent access to the 'depth' that we perceive imaginatively. We see others only through their behaviours and language: the threat of deception and misunderstand-ing, though mitigated by all sorts of factors, is always real. We can go an entire life without really knowing even those closest to us. And we see the world only through patterns inherited from our religion or culture, or supported by the communities and media with which we surround ourselves. There is no independent verification, no second world against which we can check our construals of our own: there is only a laborious and often indirect checking of our construals against those of others and testing of our pat-terns against the phenomena. Such testing requires courage and perseverance: after all, as I discussed in the first chapter, to become unsure of our frameworks is to risk our ability to move in the world. And although the honest adjustment of our frameworks should ultimately expand our possibilities in the world, it often goes the other way round, and we nar-row our frameworks in response to hurt and disorientation.

If it is true of worldviews in general that there is no wider context and no independent experience that could help us conclusively arbitrate between different ways of organizing the phenomena, then this is especially true of religious faith. On the one hand, to believe in God at all (at least in a realist sense) is to affirm Him as supremely *there*, independently of any beholder; on the other, even St Paul acknowledges that we see only 'through a glass darkly', that is, never independently of the construals of our fallible imagination.[1] This chapter is about the possibility and risks of perceiving God.

The question whether we *find* God or merely make Him (up) when we orient ourselves to the divine is one of the defining questions of modernity. Feuerbach, Wagner, Marx, Nietzsche, Freud, Heidegger, and many others have regarded belief in God as the mistaken, merely imaginative projection of human concerns onto a giant screen. This projection, they argue, is not truth-apt but illusory, and cannot find anything other than our own shadows or spectres. According to these thinkers, such projection is therefore also never stable; it succeeds imaginatively only at the cost of rational incoherence.

Many theologians have attempted to safeguard a human perception of God, a human ability to experience Him in some sense directly, by positing a particular, inalienable, or at least trustworthy 'sense' of the divine. Often, this has taken the form of something very like a distinct organ or capacity, such as the Orthodox *nous*, the Reformed *sensus divinitatis*, or Henri de Lubac's natural desire for the supernatural.[2] Sometimes, it has taken the form of a foundational mood or attunement, such as Schleiermacher's feeling of absolute dependence or Bonhoeffer's *cantus firmus*.[3] In modernity, there has also been a trend to argue that any claim of a direct experience of God is nonsensical, because God is not an inner-worldly reality of any kind, but the condition of the possibility of such realities; and that He can be perceived, if at all, only indirectly as the horizon of inner-worldly relations such as those of consciousness, justice, knowledge, or desire.[4] Although fertile, this final approach, unless held in tension with others, departs from Christian Scripture, tradition, and experience, which profess God paradoxically as at once 'the ground of our beseeching', its object, and its addressee.[5]

However theorized, there is a sense that Christian faith as I described it in the last chapter – as a form of 'depth perception' of the world – is often experientially grounded in the conviction that we can, in some form, perceive or encounter God. Forms of purely decisional faith are rare. This chapter, therefore, will explore the hypothesis that there may be no way of perceiving God that is insulated from the vagaries and vicissitudes of the ordinary senses, much less one that is wholly independent of the constructive work of imagination. Though there may be experiences of radical receptivity, even these are immediately and continuously integrated into a perception that relies on imaginative projection.[6] This does not mean that our sense of God cannot be trusted or that people of faith are radically at the mercy of their experience: the tradition offers many resources for distancing oneself from one's own perceptions. Even so, the aim even of such practices is not a permanent dissociation from one's own perception but its integration. This raises at least three questions: How is a sense of God trained? What are we led to perceive? And how do we perceive absence?

Spiritual Sensation

Contemporary psychological and anthropological research converges on the claim that if faith is partly a matter of apprehension (rather than merely of reason or will), then such apprehension utilizes pathways and processes also active in other domains of life, rather than unique or categorically distinct ones.[7] Apprehending the divine is in an important sense a matter of what, in common parlance, is called 'imagination'. As T. M. Luhrmann puts it, 'Faith is about … the ontological attitude people take toward what must be imagined – not because gods and spirits are necessarily imaginary, but because they cannot be known with the senses, and people of faith must allow those invisible others to feel alive to them.'[8]

Luhrmann argues that contrary to the former psychologists' assumption that religious people experience God as an immediate presence, in similar ways as schizophrenics experience voices or drug addicts hallucinations, they in fact have to *work* to make God present. Although the commitment to such work sometimes has roots in a radical, unbidden, and unexpected experience of divine presence – a mystical experience, a near-death experience, a conversion experience – the day-to-day experience of divine presence is a matter of practice, required in part by the fact that the term 'presence', when used of spiritual realities, necessarily functions differently from its usage for objects-in-the-world.

These claims – that our experience of God is mediated by a training of our exterior and interior senses – are consonant with the long Eastern theological tradition of spiritual sensation, though the modern psychological approach, as well as my own account of the imagination, raise acute questions which that tradition has not yet answered. (More on these later on.) The tradition of spiritual sensation, which reaches us from Origen, Gregory of Nyssa, and Maximus, claims that our perceptive and emotional apparatus is by no means fixed, but is malleable and trainable, and must be shaped by habit and the Holy Spirit to see the world aright. In the West, this tradition has been rediscovered and passed on by the great mid twentieth-century Ressourcement theologians, including Hans Urs von Balthasar, Jean Daniélou, and Henri de Lubac.[9]

The spiritual senses tradition, as Sarah Coakley describes it, 'represents an approach to human sensual, perceptual, and accompanying moral capacities as labile and malleable, according to their congruence with the graced and purifying work of God, the Holy Spirit':[10]

> Even our ordinary human perceptions or sensations of the world are not simply available to us on a universally-given epistemic 'flat-plane', so to speak; for they are subject to certain transformations, both negative and positive, according – on the one hand – to graced spiritual transitions in the realm of sanctification, but also – on the other – to negative factors of bad habit, manipulation or even corruption.[11]

Thus, Origen argues that the individual development of our five senses towards refinement and sensitivity to Christ is not a matter of instantaneous conversion but the undertaking of a lifetime.[12]

The spiritual senses tradition responds to the recognition that our awareness of God (and of the world as related to God) is not insulated from the vagaries of the human senses, but relies on them; and that the senses are not stably registering reality as it is, but are malleable, both by sin and the world and by divine inspiration. This is an extension of the classical understanding of the *ordo amoris*, 'the

te condition of the affections in which every object
rded that kind of degree of love which is appropriate
.. .. ' For the spiritual senses tradition, the affections are
not merely a matter of liking but of seeing: to be virtuous,
to love well, is to *see* things *as* what they truly are, according them the value they truly have. This requires a training of one's perception just as it does of one's will; and it
is therefore a perceptual rather than just an ethical task to
expose oneself and one's children to God, his word and his
church, in such a way as to form one's sensual apparatus to
see things aright.

For most of Western history, such perceptual training
was one of the main justifications for creating and receiv-
ing art, music, and literature. As late as the late nineteenth
century, the study of English literature was widely defended
as necessary 'to correct the taste [and] to strengthen the
judgement'.[14] This defence was a commonplace of classical
educational theory: 'To like and dislike the proper things –
this is what good education means', Aristotle writes after
Plato.[15] 'When the age for reflective thought comes', C. S.
Lewis elaborates, 'the pupil who has been thus trained in
"ordinate affections" or "just sentiments"' – who has come
to discern beauty in a landscape painting, to love noble
characters and despise base ones – 'will easily find the first
principles in Ethics.'[16] This is part of why Aslan can comfort Edmund and Lucy by saying, 'This was the very reason
why you were brought to Narnia, that by knowing me here
for a little, you may know me better there.'[17]

Extending the language of imagination used in this book
so far, we might say that religious awareness moves on a

spectrum which is familiar to us from the domain of 'taste' or expertise: A skilled wine taster or a skilled reader of poetry has practised his or her perceptual skills to discern in the nose of a wine or the inflections of a poem nuances that may be *there*, but require an acquired taste or a trained sensitivity to smell and see. Likewise, spiritual perception requires a taste for God, which may not be static, but change and develop.[18] Both aesthetic and spiritual engagement, however, require a basic *trust* in life, as wine tasting requires a trust in the complexity and goodness of wine, and literary criticism of the old schools (most recently New Criticism) requires a trust that a poem is load-bearing: that it can bear and repay interpretative investment.[19]

Transposition

The question before us – how, if at all, do we perceive God? – is, in a sense, significantly more complicated than the aesthetic analogy makes it seem. To taste a good wine is a kind of depth perception: there is more to this drink than meets the untrained eye. Its pleasure is, in fact, remarkably akin to the pleasure of metaphor: it is the pleasure of tasting in one liquid the notes of fruit, minerals, and vegetation that in most of life have their own, disparate existence – to draw and perceive the connections between things (in this case mediated by similar chemical structures). This shows a kind of depth to the world, a depth at which things are related to each other and we to them.

But the connections are nevertheless between things that exist, in some sense, within the same reality: herbs, animals, humans. Faith, by contrast, demands a perceptual training to see depth of a completely different kind, a depth that exceeds the nature of earthly things, that is, in the scholastic sense of the term, supernatural. Simply to say, with the classical spiritual senses tradition or classic Aristotelianism, that to see aright is to accord all things their proper place and value, is not, within the terms of this book, a viable solution. No matter how deeply we believe in God, we cannot simply equate true vision with a vision that accords to all things their proper value within the irreducible multiplicity of the world. (This is one of the implications of Chapter 1 and, I would say, one of the central difficulties of Lewis's *Abolition of Man*.[20]) However, if it is neither a depth perception strictly analogous to that of aesthetic taste, nor a strict adjustment of perception to an agreed pattern, how can we speak of spiritual perception?

The literary scholar and Christian philosopher C. S. Lewis is, on this question, one of the most unassumingly profound thinkers of the twentieth century. Much of his thought on the imagination was developed before his conversion to Christianity in studies of the complex dialectics of desire and a critical correspondence with Owen Barfield on the capacities and failures of imagination.[21] In a paper of 1945 (originally delivered as a sermon in Oxford), Lewis outlines a theory of the senses that likens the perception of spiritual realities to a sort of depth-perception familiar from art. Whereas I have been discussing the imaginative work of integrating undifferentiated sense impressions into patterns or forms, Lewis confronts just the problem that I want to get into view, namely how to even speak about perceiving a depth that lies beyond the dimensions of the perceptible world.

Beginning from Paul's discourse on glossolalia in 1 Corinthians 14, Lewis enquires into the fact that although speaking in tongues may sometimes be nothing but a hysterical phenomenon, it cannot categorically be dismissed as hysteria by Christians who take St Paul seriously. Lewis analogizes this to the frequent association of mystical experiences with erotic feelings and language, which may sometimes be forms of sublimation but cannot be reduced to them without remainder. To find a surer ground for arbitration, Lewis analogizes these further to less spiritual, more everyday experiences that exhibit similar patterns. Thus, he observes that different, even contrasting states of his soul often express themselves in the *same* bodily sensations; his example is a kind of kick or flutter in the diaphragm which is his response to both 'very bad news' and 'the overture of *The Magic Flute*'. In one context, the internal flutter is a pleasure; in another, a misery. 'It is not a mere sign of joy and anguish: it becomes what it signifies. When the joy thus flows over into the nerves, that overflow is its consummation: when the anguish thus flows over that physical symptom is the crowning horror.'[22]

Lewis concludes:

I take our emotional life to be 'higher' than the life of our sensations – ... richer, more varied, more subtle. And this is a higher level which nearly all of us know. And I believe that if anyone watches carefully the relation between his emotions and his sensations he will discover the following facts; (1) that the nerves do respond, and in a sense most adequately and exquisitely, to the emotions; (2) that their resources are far more limited, the possible variations of sense far fewer, than those of emotion; (3) and that the senses compensate for this by using the *same* sensation to express more than one emotion – even, as we have seen, to express opposite emotions.[23]

On this theory, physical states become a repertoire or language mediating experiences that exceed physicality, yet cannot be experienced independently of it. This may occur in psychosomatic illnesses, in which bodies express what souls suffer, often in body parts that the community associates with relevant aspects of the inner life: heartache, head strain, an upset stomach. It may also occur in states of emotional excitement, in which one may experience goosebumps, burn as with fever, or feel butterflies in one's stomach. These physical states express or mediate psychological states that are in some sense coextensive with them, yet in another exceed and lend them significance. Bodily sensations, even basic emotions, for Lewis, are simple instruments mediating a wide range of realities – pianos transposing orchestral scores.

In this elasticity, sensations resemble language, which (for Lewis as for later theorists such as George Lakoff, Mark Johnson, and their many followers) similarly describes experiences that exceed physicality primarily through the figurative use of words whose original referent is physical.[24] 'That was heavy' is used to refer not only to a suitcase, but also to a dense lecture or to a bitter funeral (where 'dense' and 'bitter', too, have their origins in physical realities). This multivalent use of a single term is not a form of logical categorization (like the generalizing use of a single term 'pet' to refer to both cats and dogs): suitcases and funerals do not fall within the same experiential or logical category independently of a term such as 'heavy'. At the same time, such multivalent use of language cannot be reduced to a purer, univocal use that identifies non-physical phenomena by purely abstract words; as Lakoff, Johnson, Mary Gerhart, Allan Russell, and many others have shown, there are no such words.[25]

One of the challenges highlighted by these accounts is that it is not possible to identify a phenomenon of the soul or spirit simply by pointing at a discrete entity and saying, 'look! there!'. Lewis illustrates the challenge vividly by the thought experiment of convincing a two-dimensional being that a certain triangular shape in a picture represents a road receding in the distance. No difference identifiable within a two-dimensional reference frame distinguishes the road from a flat triangular shape, and no appeal to a putative third dimension in which this distinction makes sense could be comprehensible to a two-dimensional creature.[26] For Lewis, this fictional scenario resembles a common predicament. One cannot simply point a doctor or scientist to a pang in the heart and say 'this is grief'. In his instruments, it will show up the same way as a cardiac pain. Instead, to suggest that there is a three-dimensional road rather than a two-dimensional triangle, or an ailment of the soul rather than merely a malfunction of the body, one must point out things that are odd or remain unexplained within the merely material context. Why does the flutter of the stomach arise in this situation? Why does this fever appear as pleasurable? Why is this desire not satisfied by any ordinary joy, despite the fact that the person experiencing it is not someone known to be permanently dissatisfied?[27]

Seeing Presence, Seeing Absence

We search for psychological or spiritual depth partly because the realities we encounter present themselves to us as incomplete within their own dimensions, and therefore as indicative of more than meets the eye. If this is the case, then one way of suggesting that we, others, and the world have unseen depth is by pointing out things that remain incomplete or incoherent within a merely material, or even a merely psychological or sociological, context. This is a basic impetus of both art and religion. It is another dimension of Rowan Williams's observation, already quoted in Chapter 3, that the reality we encounter 'is obscurely incomplete'; that it 'proposes to the poet the task of making it significant – which does not mean imposing upon it an alien structure of explanation'.[28] Williams, like Maritain, notes an incompleteness to our merely physical experience of the world, which both art and faith register and respond to faithfully and creatively.

However, this unseen depth is mediated by imagination and desire, which are fallible. This is as true of the interpretation of art (which is perpetually fraught with the anxiety of over-interpretation) as it is of the experience of the divine. In striving to perceive God, the burden of interpretative responsibility and its endemic risk of error cannot be circumvented by relying, as Plantinga's *sensus divinitatis* attempts, on a special mechanism which is insulated against the vagaries of the ordinary senses.[29] Neither can it be cut short by the experience of 'saturated phenomena' – phenomena which, as in Jean-Luc Marion's vision, overwhelm us from outside our own intentional movements. Such experiences of overwhelm certainly occur, but they must nevertheless be assimilated into everyday life through conscious self-orientation and interpretation. And because experience of the divine in our own selves and the world relies on imaginative investment, it is impossible categorically to avoid its over- or misinterpretation. Perceptions of God, even for those who firmly believe in the divine, are always vulnerable to over-narration (think of the convalescent, in disregard of those who have died of the same illness, declaring that 'God healing me proved his love for me'), to disconfirmation (think of the disillusioned charismatic bitterly reporting that 'what I thought was plenitude was really manipulation'), and to repeated re-narration (think of anyone who has experienced failed vocations or relationships).

This raises with renewed force the question of what it is that spiritual vision sees. On the one hand, it takes the form of an enriched depth perception: an apprehension of a depth of intention, significance, beauty, or connection in and among ordinary things. These forms of awareness are mediated by a trained imagination and trained desire. On the other hand, spiritual vision may confront us with incompleteness and disjunction that are not easily resolved at any depth accessible to us: contradictions that drive us beyond any attempt to make sense of life within its own dimensions, and cannot be made coherent even by the depth projection of divine providence.

This dynamic is at work in any apprehension of eternity within human finitude that resists both a premature arrogation of participation in plenitude and a denial that such participation can be coherently desired. It is well illustrated in Edith Stein's theological critique of Heidegger's claim not only that to be fully human is to live in the face of death, but also (and this is the claim she rejects) that we can truly experience the dread of death only by anticipating our own death, never by witnessing another's. Stein insists that, on the contrary, it is precisely the death of others – especially that of loved ones – which brings us most radically face to face with finitude.[30] Only in the light of love for another does death appear as the horrendous negation it is. This is because to love, as Heidegger himself realized in reflecting on his love for Hannah Arendt, is to say *'volo ut sis'* – 'I want you to be'.[31]

This desire, so basic to love, that life should be infinite need not be an immodest rejection of life's finitude. Rather, it may be a humble acknowledgement of the simultaneous undeniability and impossibility of an imaginatively mediated vision. Theology demands not that people of faith make sense of this contradiction, but that they acknowledge it. The New Testament is full of baffling images of eternal life: seeing not through a glass darkly but face to face; being raised as a seed is raised or born as a child is born. These suggest not that eternal life is simply an unending continuation of life in the form in which we know it, but rather that it relates to life as reality relates to image, plant to seed, a fully grown human to an embryo. These images, in other words, put us in the position of C. S.

Lewis's two-dimensional creatures, dimly apprehending a third dimension beyond the limits of any possible imagination. If these images are in any way load-bearing, then the experience of unresolvable contradiction or bafflement is precisely adequate, because clinging simply to a conviction of the continuation of life as we know it would not in fact answer to the desire.

Mystics witness to the fact that the bafflement of this contradiction – the incompleteness and incoherence of life within its own dimensions – may itself open into an encounter with God. A disciple of Edith Stein captures this viscerally after separation from a loved one:

> Such impossible desire for another person leads me to the place beyond the possible where union would be but cannot be. In that place, I experience that utter poverty in which alone I am aware of the desirability of the world without being enthralled to it, and aware of its insufficiency without being disdainful of it. In short, I experience the condition of standing as a creature before God who is at once creator, judge and saviour. I stand in this poverty, extending my arms in puzzlement, unable to speak, merely nonsensically repeating, 'I miss her, I miss her.' This desire can be neither replaced nor fulfilled: I have nothing but my love and the admission that it cannot be lived. To stand in this impossibility – to stand without ground to stand on – is to stand before God.[32]

A life of faith is not merely a way of making sense of the world. It is also a way of acknowledging the nonsensicality of the world: neither to deny nor prematurely to resolve it. Engaging this dimension of faith requires a self-abnegating imagination, that is, an imagination that knows itself to be at once necessary and constitutively inadequate. Such imagination is trained on intentional attention to the things that are odd: to the gaps in human experience that do not and will not make sense.

The human vocation is to be drawn, at the last, into the triune life of God: that love between Father, Son, and Spirit which defines the divine nature or life and overflows into the creation of a non-divine world. However, such 'deification' is not a calling that is attainable by human capacities. This is because 'to be like God' does not consist (as Adam and Eve were tempted into believing in the Genesis story) in achieving autonomy, but in being drawn, as Thomas Aquinas puts it, 'above the condition of [our] nature to a participation of the Divine good'.[33] Therefore, although 'man by his nature is ordained to beatitude as his end', he is ordained to *attain* this end 'not by his own strength', but only by the 'help of grace', which draws him into the love of God.[34]

This vision of humans as existentially incomplete complicates what we might say about spiritual vision, because it bespeaks a restlessness that is not contingent, but remains constitutive of our existence in this world. And yet if the human desire for completion does not find fulfilment within the world, neither does it stand over against it: all human relationships of love anticipate it, and all care for the world prepares for it. 'This also is thou – neither is this thou', as Charles Williams says after the Vedas.[35] This way, which is both a way of affirmation and a way of negation, is the way we make in hope; and it cannot be asserted – it can only be lived.

Notes

1. 1 Corinthians 13.12 (King James Version).
2. See e.g. Gregory Palamas, 'On the Blessed Hesychasts,' in *Early Fathers from the Philokalia: Together with Some Writings of St. Abba Dorotheus, St. Isaac of Syria, and St. Gregory Palamas*, translated by E. Kadloubovsky and G. E. H. Palmer (London: Faber, 1954), 401–409; John Romanides, *Patristic Theology* (Thessaloniki: Uncut Mountain Press, 2008), 19–23; Alvin Plantinga, *Warranted Christian Belief* (Oxford: Oxford University Press, 2000); Henri de Lubac, *Surnaturel: Études historiques* (Paris: Aubier, 1946).
3. See Friedrich Schleiermacher, *Reden über die Religion: an die Gebildeten unter ihren Verächtern* (Gotha: Friedrich Andreas Perthes, 1799), translated by Richard Crouter as *On Religion: Speeches to Its Cultured Despisers* (Cambridge: Cambridge University Press, 1988), ch. 2; and Schleiermacher, *Glaubenslehre* (Gotha: Friedrich Andreas Perthes, 2nd ed., 1831), translated by H. R. Mackintosh and J. S. Stewart as *The Christian Faith* (Edinburgh: T&T Clark, 1928); Dietrich Bonhoeffer, *Widerstand und Ergebung: Briefe und Aufzeichnungen aus der Haft* (Munich: Christian Kaiser, 2nd ed., 1970), translated by Isabel Best as *Letters and Papers from Prison* (Minneapolis, MN: Fortress Press, 2010), 394.
4. Descartes, Kant, Hegel, Rahner, de Lubac.
5. Julian of Norwich, *Revelations of Divine Love*, edited by Barry Windeatt (Oxford: Oxford University Press, 2015), ch. 41.
6. In contemporary writing, see e.g. Brian D. Robinette, *The Difference Nothing Makes* (South Bend, IN: Notre Dame University Press, 2023), ch. 5; and Martin Laird, *Into the Silent Land* (London: Darton, Longman & Todd, 2006), for moving accounts of radical receptivity within Christian contemplative practice.

7. See e.g. Uffe Schjødt and Marc Andersen, 'How Does Religious Experience Work in Predictive Minds?,' *Religion, Brain & Behavior* 7, no. 4 (2017): 320–333; Uffe Schjødt, 'Predictive Coding in the Study of Religion,' *Supplements to Method & Theory in the Study of Religion* 13 (2019), 364–379; T. M. Luhrmann, *How God Becomes Real: Kindling the Presence of Invisible Others* (Princeton, NJ: Princeton University Press, 2020).

8. Luhrmann, *How God Becomes Real*, 79.

9. See e.g. Mark McInroy, *Balthasar on the Spiritual Senses: Perceiving Splendour* (Oxford: Oxford University Press, 2014); Fred Aquino and Gabriel Gavrilyuk (eds), *Perceiving Things Divine: Towards a Constructive Account of Spiritual Perception* (Oxford: Oxford University Press, 2022); Sarah Coakley, *Sensing God? Reconsidering the Patristic Doctrine of 'Spiritual Sensation' for Contemporary Theology and Ethics*, The Père Marquette Lecture 2022 (Milwaukee, WI: Marquette University Press, 2022).

10. Coakley, *Sensing God?*, 3.

11. Coakley, *Sensing God?*, 3.

12. Coakley, *Sensing God?*, 6.

13. C. S. Lewis, *The Abolition of Man* (Oxford: Oxford University Press, 1943), 16.

14. H. J. Rose, 'The Duty of Maintaining the Truth,' Sermon to the University of Cambridge, 1834, quoted by Stefan Collini, 'Beauty and the Footnote, Lecture 1: Justifications,' University of St Andrews, 11 October 2022.

15. Aristotle, *Nicomachean Ethics* 1104b.

16. Lewis, *Abolition of Man*, 16.

17. C. S. Lewis, *The Voyage of the Dawn Treader* (London: Geoffrey Bles, 1952), ch. 16.

18. See also the critical-comparative discussion of such training in Luhrmann, *How God Becomes Real*, ch. 3.

19. There are obvious parallels between my account and some philosophical accounts of virtue; see esp. Iris Murdoch, *The Sovereignty of the Good* (London: Routledge, 1970); Martha Nussbaum, *Upheavals of Thought: The Intelligence of Emotions* (Cambridge: Cambridge University Press, 2001).

20. See my critique in Judith Wolfe, 'Theology in *The Abolition of Man*,' in Gayne Anacker and Tim Mosteller (eds), *Contemporary Perspectives on C. S. Lewis' The Abolition of Man* (London: Bloomsbury, 2016), 97–110.

21. See e.g. C. S. Lewis (as Clive Hamilton), *Spirits in Bondage: A Cycle of Lyrics* (London: Heinemann, 1919); Owen Barfield and C. S. Lewis, *The 'Great War' of Owen Barfield and C.S. Lewis: Philosophical Writings, 1927–1930*, edited by Norbert Feinendegen and Arend Smilde, *Inklings Studies Supplements* 1 (2019).

22. C. S. Lewis, 'Transposition,' in *They Asked for a Paper: Papers and Addresses* (London: Geoffrey Bles, 1962), 166–182, p. 170. Thomas Mann gives us a darkly humorous portrayal of an advocate of the identity of emotions and sensations in Doctor Behrens: 'Stimulus is stimulus. The body doesn't give a hang for the content of the stimulus. It may be minnows, it may be the Holy Ghost, the sebaceous glands are erected just the same,' in *Der Zauberberg* (Berlin: S. Fischer, 1924), translated by T. H. Lowe-Porter as *The Magic Mountain* (London: Secker & Warburg, 1928), 264 (ch. 5). I am grateful to Thomas Pfau for the reference.

23. Lewis, 'Transposition,' 170.

24. See especially C. S. Lewis, 'Bluspels and Flalansferes: A Semantic Nightmare,' in *Rehabilitations* (London: Geoffrey Bles, 1939), 133–158; Lakoff and Johnson, *Metaphors We Live By*.

25. See Lakoff and Johnson, *Metaphors We Live By*; Mary Gerhart and Allan Russell, *Metaphoric Process: The Creation*

of Scientific and Religious Understanding (Fort Worth, TX: Texas Christian University Press, 1984).

26. See Lewis, 'Transposition,' 174–179; Lewis, 'Bluspels and Flalansferes'; Lewis, *Mere Christianity* (London: Geoffrey Bles, 1952), IV.2.

27. A profound and nuanced exploration of these questions is John Cottingham, *In Search of the Soul: A Philosophical Essay* (Princeton, NJ: Princeton University Press, 2020).

28. Williams, 'Poetic and Religious Imagination,' 179–180.

29. See Alvin Plantinga, *Warranted Christian Belief* (Oxford: Oxford University Press, 2000).

30. See Edith Stein, 'Martin Heideggers Existenzphilosophie,' in *Endliches und Ewiges Sein: Versuch eines Aufstiegs zum Sinn des Seins*, edited by Andreas Uwe Müller (Freiburg: Herder, 2006), 475–476.

31. Letters to Hannah Arendt, 13 May 1925 and 7 December 1927, in Ursula Ludz (ed.), *Hannah Arendt / Martin Heidegger: Briefe 1925–1975* (Frankfurt: Klostermann, 2nd ed., 1999), 31 and 59.

32. Elizabeth Cohen, undated, correspondence in private collection.

33. Thomas Aquinas, *Summa Theologiae* 1.110.1.

34. Aquinas, *Summa Theologiae* 2–1.114.2.

35. Charles Williams and C. S. Lewis, *Arthurian Torso* (Oxford: Oxford University Press, 1948), 151.

5 | Finding an Ending

… only in the startled space suddenly abandoned
by a nearly divine youth, the void was moved to that
vibration which now enraptures and comforts and helps us.

Rilke, 'First Duino Elegy'

The Dialectics of Eschatology

The end of the last chapter began to shift from a phenomenological to a systematic theology: the outline of
an ontological account within which the striving of the
imagination towards wholeness, as well as its continual
frustration, make sense. The conclusion held out a theological hope that the aporia of our imaginative construals
of the world – their irreducible multiplicity, their endless
revisability, their incompleteness, or (worse) mere illusion
of completeness – do not expose a reality that is senseless
or wholly subject to construction. Rather, that they tes-
tify to the incompleteness of the world: not a contingent
incompleteness – the mere absence of the last digits in a
sequence – but one that defies completion on its own terms
and requires divine action. This hope, which is a form of

eschatology, cannot be read off the structure of the human imagination; however, it can suggest one way of living with it, a way that makes sense in the light of eschatological hope.

All of Christian theology is oriented eschatologically: 'I believe in … the communion of saints, the forgiveness of sins, the resurrection of the body, and the life everlasting.'[1] This eschatological orientation has two contrasting aspects. On the one hand, the Christian faith tells a story of the world which assumes and anticipates certain ends (Greek *eschata*, 'last things'), whose character is revealed in the Scriptures and articulated in the theological tradition. On the other, it professes a radical openness to a future, a new creation, that is not yet realized and which nothing we do can bring under our imaginative or practical control.

Both aspects of eschatology are essential to Christianity. On the one hand, the Christian faith casts a vision of both individual life and of history as having direction, purpose, a story: as moving towards *ends* and an *end*. Rather than an endless cycle of suffering, as the ancient Greeks or Indians envisioned it, the Christian world is the gift of a creator, who has crafted it with love and purpose, diaphanous to him and striving for communion with him. The history of creation, fall, redemption, sanctification, and consummation gives structure both to human life and to all of history – a structure that offers orientation, purpose, and hope.

Yet on the other hand, the Christian faith professes that this consummation can only come as gift. It propounds the initially troubling (but ultimately deeply comforting) anthropology that humans are at once oriented towards

THE DIALECTICS OF ESCHATOLOGY

a supernatural end and incapable of reaching that end by their own power.[2] The story of redemption is one of repeated divine intervention: the coming of the Messiah; God's promise to 'make all things new'. The 'new creation' of the Book of Revelation is not the realization or perfection of a potential latent in the present order; it is a promise of transformation. The story, in other words, is not one that unfolds on a single plane, and it is not surprising that many theologians have drawn meta-literary or meta-theatrical analogies in describing it. 'When the author walks on to the stage', writes C. S. Lewis, 'the play is over'.[3]

The unique register of most of the Bible's eschatological passages is, I think, consonant with this duality. It is a register that simultaneously attracts and repels imaginative sense-making. It is accidental neither that the Bible speaks about eschatology most often in images, nor that these images do not readily cohere. Indeed, the Scriptures include a whole range of eschatological images, many in tension with each other. Besides the familiar images of divine judgement,[4] many images are of return or restoration: the return of Israel to Zion,[5] the reconstruction of the Temple,[6] the homecoming of each to his or her own vine and fig tree.[7] In constructive tension with these homecomings, some images are of radically new experiences or realities: ascent to the divine throne,[8] the opening of sealed books,[9] the descent of the heavenly Jerusalem.[10] Most striking are those images, perhaps most characteristic of New Testament eschatology, which hold a tension between return and novelty: images of a fulfilment that is also radically new and thus redefines what came before it. These include images of a child being born,[11] of seed springing to flower,[12] of seeing no longer in a dark mirror but now face to face.[13]

These latter images, in particular, both invite and defy imagination. Like the text of the Apocalypse of St John, they are not so much ciphers for decoding the 'signs of the times' (as apocalyptic politics and sects would wish) as channels for directing desire. The coda of the Apocalypse draws its readers into a continuing interplay of voices calling for each other's presence: 'And the Spirit and the Bride say, Come. And let him that heareth say, Come ... Surely I come quickly. Amen. Even so, come, Lord Jesus.'[14] These are expressions not of knowledge but of longing. As Chapter 4 suggested, such eschatological longing can be understood as a form of self-abnegating imagination, corresponding to the dialectics of Christian eschatology. It responds both to the glimpse of a vision that makes sense of the world and of life, and to the realization that this vision cannot be firmly secured within the conditions of the world and thus remains, in some sense, beyond imaginative reach.

To put it differently, the eschatological images of birth, seed, and discarded mirrors imaginatively project a passage from one form of reality to another, and identify our present life with the poorer of the two: with an embryo still unborn, a seed still unsprung, a person who knows only images, not realities. To identify ourselves with this condition is, indeed, an imaginative exercise; but to imagine it earnestly is to realize the impossibility of further or more concrete imaginings of the end. Seed and embryo cannot claim to know what they will be; they can only desire a

THE DIALECTICS OF ESCHATOLOGY

fulfilment that they cannot yet fully fathom. If the eschatological images of Romans 8 and 1 Corinthians 13 and 15 enable any form of imaginative sight, it has the character not of knowledge but of desire.

This complicates the relationship between faith and art. For precisely inasmuch as works of art offer clarity and closure, they are both inspiring and potentially deceptive. They are deceptive when we try to take them as blueprints for arranging our lives. Life does not (for the most part) end in a climactic death that makes sense of and crowns all that has gone before it, like Don Quixote's or Jean Valjean's; it ends awkwardly, with difficulty. And although the attempt to make out of life a coherent story is, in some senses, necessary to living meaningfully, it is also, as we saw in Chapter 2, a fraught business, leading to wilful exclusions and blindnesses, and to the need to re-narrate one's story to oneself again and again at points of crisis and failure. Likewise, history has no stable, unfolding plot, only a myriad of competing stories, sometimes violently enforced, imposed with weapons or insinuated with slogans and emotional manipulation. The attempt to force history into a plot, with a happy (or, for that matter, a tragic) ending, is the poisonous root of political religions and technological utopianism.

This is part of why I argued in Chapter 3 that the images and stories of art do not serve as *models* of ordinary life but as something like second lenses or descants. In this chapter, I will extend and concretize this claim in light of the dialectics of eschatology. In doing so, I will also return to the concluding discussion of Chapter 2 about the ways

Shakespeare's and Beckett's plays make us conscious of their own limits. As I aim to show, the subject matter of eschatology has sometimes engendered a tradition of art that is ready both to step in and to get out of the way: to cast a vision without arresting its viewers in it. I will explore some of that history, focusing, like Chapter 3, primarily on visual art, which provides the most readily accessible set of examples. I will then return to poetry and theatre. Extending the discussion of Shakespeare from Chapter 2, I will close with an account of a form of artistic imagination that shoulders the responsibility both of its adequacy and of its inadequacy to the world: an art that creates images which tend towards their own dissolution.

The Apocalypse in Art

Although some works of art depicting the Apocalypse aim merely to overwhelm, many are sensitive to the dilemma I raised in the last section. They do not so much project closure as demand that their viewers, readers, or listeners reconsider their own lives in light of realities beyond their grasp. We can see this in the history of apocalyptic painting and sculpture from the Middle Ages to modernity, which rarely aim at self-contained aesthetic experiences, but consciously relate themselves to the surrounding world.[15] In the Middle Ages, Last Judgements were often found above the main gates of large churches and cathedrals. On the tympanum of the pilgrim cathedral of Autun in Burgundy (c. AD 1130, Fig. 25), the souls

Fig. 25 Gislebertus, tympanum depicting the Last Judgement, c. 1130–1142. Stone; Cathedral of Saint Lazarus of Autun, Autun, France. Photo: Gaudry Daniel, CC BY-SA 3.0 Deed.

awaiting judgement are themselves depicted as pilgrims, bearing the shell of Santiago di Compostela or the cross of the Holy Sepulchre. This representation invites those who are concluding their pilgrimage here to imagine this journey as the journey of their lives and the cathedral gates as those of the heavenly Jerusalem. They are here to receive purification and rest before returning to their ordinary lives in the light of this experience and, perhaps, reimagining it in that light.

In other churches, Last Judgements were found at the east end, as altarpieces, frescoes, or east windows. Here, they offered a visionary frame for the real presence of Christ in the Eucharist, which (as discussed in Chapter 3) both anticipates and prepares for his *parousia*. Michelangelo's *Last*

Fig. 26 Michelangelo, *The Last Judgement*, 1536–1541. Fresco, 370 × 1200 cm; Sistine Chapel, Rome, Vatican City.

Judgement (1536–41, Fig. 26) takes place in a painted sky towering above the altar of the Sistine Chapel. Unlike the ceiling, which occupies its own artistic world, this fresco abrogates any boundaries between the world of this judgement and that of the worshippers. The sky – this-worldly and full of storm clouds – rises directly over the altar, and the figures are so hyper-corporeal that the weight of the

Fig. 27 Detail of Michelangelo, *The Last Judgement*, 1536–1541. Fresco, 370 × 1200 cm; Sistine Chapel, Rome, Vatican City.

saved must be dragged upward and the angels are without wings (Fig. 27). And although Christ is framed by sunlight (Fig. 28), the entire painting appears illuminated directly from the front, that is, from the western end of the church, as if the sun were setting on the world. The damned find with horrified surprise that they have made their decision without knowing it (Fig. 29). Like Rilke's Apollo, this Christ, though his eyes are averted, issues a direct imperative: 'You must change your life.'[16]

The art of Autun and the Sistine Chapel assumes an inherited eschatology and – like Dante, Giotto, Signorelli, and Memling (Fig. 30) – strives to visualize a future that casts its light on the world unseen. By the nineteenth

Fig. 28 Detail of Michelangelo, *The Last Judgement*, 1536–1541.
Fresco, 370 × 1200 cm; Sistine Chapel, Rome, Vatican City.

century, the underpinning religious consensus had
waned, and people increasingly looked to art to bring
about rather than to prophesy eschatological fulfilment.

136

Fig. 29 Detail of Michelangelo, *The Last Judgement*, 1536–1541. Fresco, 370 × 1200 cm; Sistine Chapel, Rome, Vatican City.

Fig. 30 Hans Memling, *The Last Judgement Triptych*, 1467–1471.
Oil on panel, 241.0 × 180.8 cm (central panel), 242.0 × 90.0 cm
(side panels); National Museum, Gdańsk, Poland.

Last Judgements such as those by William Blake or
John Martin were installed not in religious but in secular spaces, where they were intended to transform the
viewers' ordinary experience. Blake's *Vision of the Last
Judgement* (1808, Fig. 31) teems with a multitude of figures whose movement creates the impression of a human
skull. It is in the human head that Blake imagines the last
judgement to take place – not as the final act of history,
directed by an external authority, but as an apocalyptic
transformation of the mind. 'If the spectator could enter
into these images in his imagination', he writes about the
painting, 'approaching them on the fiery chariot of his
contemplative thought, … then would he arise from the
grave.'[17]

Fig. 31 William Blake, *A Vision of the Last Judgement*, 1808.
Pencil, ink, and watercolour, 51.0 × 39.5 cm; Petworth House,
West Sussex, UK.

This confidence did not last long. Two World Wars
exposed the utopian or messianic dreams of European, especially German, civilization as catastrophic delusions. Artists

Fig. 32 Ernst Ludwig Kirchner, *Apokalypse II (Saint John's Vision of the Seven Candlesticks)*, 1917. Watercolour; Ernst Ludwig Kirchner Sketchbooks, 1917–1932, Ernst Ludwig Kirchner Letters and Papers, Getty Library, Los Angeles, USA. Credit: The Getty Research Institute, Los Angeles (850463).

therefore forcefully rejected visions of eschatological wholeness and, instead, saw it as their responsibility to exercise a self-imposed weakness, expressing a commitment to reality in its chafing incoherence. The biblical illustrations of Ernst Ludwig Kirchner (1917, Fig. 32), Heinrich Vogeler (1918,

Fig. 33), and Max Beckmann (1941–42, Fig. 34) cast the apocalypse as a symbol not of consummation but of rupture and eschatological hope as ineradicable self-delusion.[18] Gentler modern apocalypses such as Sidney Spencer's *Resurrection in Cookham* (1924–27, Fig. 35) see the eschaton not as transcending the ordinary but as effecting reconciliation with it.

In the past century, the West's relationship to eschatology has been further complicated by the fact that matters hitherto confined to the religious imagination have increasingly come within reach of practical possibility. They include unprecedented destruction: the devastation of the world through atomic weapons, depletion of resources, or human-influenced climate change; and the annihilation of cultures by economic, technological, or medical disasters spreading unstoppably through a closely connected globe. Conversely, they promise the possibility of a 'brave new world' through death-defeating human enhancement or artificial super-intelligence. These ever-accelerating possibilities have engendered a widespread and inchoate apocalyptic imagination in late twentieth- and early twenty-first-century politics, culture, and art. In the arts, this continues to be expressed in imagery drawn directly from the Bible (such as the rapture in Tom Perrotta's *The Leftovers*),[19] but also extends to other broadly apocalyptic imagery. The increasing popularity of apocalyptic and post-apocalyptic fiction in literature, film, and television – including Perrotta, Cormac McCarthy, Emily St John Mandel, and many others[20] – reflects the need for art to allow audiences imaginatively and emotionally to explore a sense of living at the end of the world as we know it.

Fig. 33 Heinrich Vogeler, *The Seven Bowls of Wrath*, 1918. Etching on Simili-Japon, 36.3 × 26.0 cm; private collection. Photo: The Picture Art Collection / Alamy Stock Photo.

Fig. 34 Max Beckmann, *Apokalypse*, c. 1941–1942. Lithograph, 25.5 × 17 cm. In *Johannes, Offenbarung (Kapitel 6, Verse 1–8) 8.* Illustration aus dem Buch 'Apokalypse'. Credit: bpk / Sprengel Museum Hannover, Schenkung Bernhard und Margit Sprengel, Hannover (1965) / Stefan Behrens.

Fig. 35 Stanley Spencer, *The Resurrection, Cookham*, 1924–1927. Oil on canvas, 274.3 × 548.6 cm; Tate, London, UK. Credit: Tate.

There and Back Again

In all these cases, artists draw on apocalyptic imagery to effect an interruption, often violent or confusing, of our habituated imagination of the world, and thus to alter our ways of seeing and relating to it. Their approaches are grounded in a wide range of intuitions about the world: of what is true and what is necessary. However, they converge on a sense that to change the world, it is necessary to reimagine it, and to reimagine it, it is sometimes necessary to undergo an aesthetic experience. Visual art is a powerful medium because it can, in a sense, recreate the visionary clarity and intensity of the apocalyptic visions themselves, and so irrupt directly into the narrative of a life.[21]

However, as the examples of Perrotta, McCarthy, and St John Mandel suggest, eschatological expectation or apocalyptic consciousness is also and profoundly a matter of how we relate to time. And although visual images can affect or relativize our sense of time by puncturing it, they do not share the quality of temporal change that defines our own experiences of longing and fear. Visual art has borders, but not endings. Literature and music, by contrast, affect our consciousness of time precisely by sharing and remoulding it from within. To read, hear, or watch texts, music, or theatre is always to be moving towards their end, and this experience is itself part of their transformative work.[22] Dante conceived the *Divine Comedy* in part as a way to undergo an imaginative experience of hell in life so as to avoid its literal experience after death. Reading the many iterations of the Faust myth, the great Russian novels, or the fantasies of George MacDonald, J. R. R. Tolkien, Peter S. Beagle, or Ursula LeGuin does not leave our relation to time and death unchanged.

The gestalt shifts enabled by literature or music, in other words, are not immediate or all-at-once, as encounters with a great painting can be. They demand movement in time: the accumulation of a history with and within a literary, theatrical, or musical world. In a sense, this is nowhere handled more masterfully than in Richard Wagner's motive-structured operas. 'A Wagnerian motive (leitmotif)', in Roger Scruton's words, 'is a fragment of music with a memory. It retains and transforms its remembered input as the drama unfolds.'[23] The great apocalyptic moments of Wagner's art – the apotheosis of Tristan and Isolde, the divestment and later the immolation of Brünnhilde – achieve their almost inexpressible pathos by gathering up and transforming leitmotifs that have gathered a weight of history over five or, in the latter case, twenty hours of opera.

In doing so, Wagner's *Tristan* and *Ring* transform their listeners' experience of time, and create their own eschatology.[24] However, notwithstanding their brilliance, these works are also counter-examples to the eschatological art I have been discussing, because they have something of an ouroboric quality. Wagner's aim seems to be, in an important sense, not to point a way back to ordinary life but to compete with it: he creates *Gesamtkunstwerke* which, like trompe l'œil paintings, feign a completeness that is sustained only by a forced perspective.[25] Even if Brünnhilde's ungodding is a gesture towards the succession of the gods by humans, they are humans who thrive only in and on their own art.

Consider, by contrast, the ending of T. S. Eliot's *Four Quartets*, when, at the end of a long sojourn, 'the fire and the rose are one'. Like Wagner, Eliot figures a kind of apocalypse that relies on the accumulated history of his chosen motives. In the *Quartets*, too, it is only by following the poems' developing imagery of paths, of roses, and of fire – by internalizing the dimensions of these images and absorbing the loss, severity, and devouring force that they severally signify in the poems – that the culminating melding of these images can open something in its readers, can knit things together, can come as a revelation. For '[w]hat we call the beginning is often the end / And to make an end is to make a beginning. / The end is where we start from.'

Yet unlike the ending of *Tristan* or the *Ring*, the revelation at the end of the *Quartets* cannot be contained in the

poem; it impels its readers to repeat the poem's movement
in life:

> With the drawing of this Love and the voice of this calling
> We shall not cease from exploration
> And the end of all our exploring
> Will be to arrive where we started
> And know the place for the first time.

The destination of this movement is not guaranteed by
the poem; its meaning is as much beyond the poem, perhaps, as love is beyond desire. Yet it may be that the poem
has awakened a courage to hope for it. This movement of
'there and back again' echoes that of the Mass,[26] which
is named after its imperative to go out: *Ite, missa est.* The
poem becomes, in Heidegger's term, a formal indication to
a path that can only be walked in ordinary life.

The End of Images

There is one further step to take. I began the chapter by
arguing that Christian eschatology inspires and requires
a self-abnegating imagination, one that embodies a radical openness to a consummation that can ultimately only
arrive as gift. To present any merely constructed reality
as an achievement of such consummation (whether it be
a political utopia or a Wagnerian opera) is to betray this
fundamental insight. A key moment of eschatological
art or imagination as I have described it, therefore, is the
need to return to ordinary life in the light of an apocalyptic or epiphanic experience: a return from the Mount of

Transfiguration or the garden of Jesus's tomb. *Noli me tangere. Ite, missa est.*

In visual art, this is most naturally effected by the conscious placement of a work within the context of ordinary exchanges: the entrance to a cathedral, the altar wall of a church. Visual art has borders, and we move around them. In literary and musical art, it can be achieved by creating an experience whose end is porous to ordinary life. Literary art has endings, and we move towards and beyond them.

However, the logic of eschatology interrogates not only what comes *after* the epiphanic moment, but also the possibility of such apocalyptic insight itself. As suggested in Chapter 4 and again in the first section of this chapter, the substance of eschatological hope remains, in some sense, not accidentally but constitutively beyond our grasp. Artists may draw directly on biblical imagery, relying in part on their textual authority and tradition of interpretation; but the artists' realization and deployment of this imagery always confronts the question not only of authority but also of legibility. Is the mystery of the future open to sight?

In Chapter 2, I suggested that such eschatological mystery in some sense surrounds each person. In the biblical imagery, eschatological fulfilment is, among other things, the realization of selfhood: birth, flowering, encounter. As long as these are unrealized, so are we: 'Beloved, we are God's children now; what we will be has not yet been revealed. What we do know is this: when he is revealed, we will be like him, for we will see him as he is.'[27] '[Y]our life is hidden with Christ in God.'[28] Personhood, in this eschatological configuration, is as much beyond any insight into one's authentic self as it is beyond any role one might play.

Samuel Beckett confronts the riddle of personhood by a radical theatrical apophaticism. As discussed in Chapter 2, he brings us face to face with the inadequacy of the achievable, and gestures towards something so completely beyond both the work and the world that we can only apprehend it by its absence. While *Not I* and *Play* concern characters arrested in the past and present, *Waiting for Godot* and *Endgame* do so precisely in relationship to an expected and never-arriving arrival or end.[29]

Shakespeare, at least near the end of his corpus, is more cataphatic than Beckett. Nevertheless, when it comes to eschatological themes, his plays consciously present themselves as both vision *and* illusion. ('Is this the promised end? Or image of that horror?' as Kent and Edgar ask in his darkest apocalypse, *King Lear*.[30]) They embody an intuition about how the world might end; yet this can never be more than an image, and as such precisely part of the order of images that is to pass away. In his late plays, which gather up and move beyond both his comedies and his tragedies, Shakespeare responds to the aporia of eschatological art by enabling a journey towards eschatological fulfilment that is both compelling and self-consciously ephemeral: he creates images that tend towards their own dissolution. He draws us into eschatological visions that are not contained by either the artwork or the ordinary world, but remain beyond their grasp.

I began considering Shakespeare's late plays in Chapter 2. There, I noted his exploration of both the power of roles and their inadequacy. We need to be present to each other by playing a role in each other's lives; but we need also to relinquish too firm a sense of presence. Shakespeare sustains this dialectic by writing magnificent roles while keeping the theatricality of these roles in view by making us release them. This is also true of world-making more generally. To orient ourselves in the world, we need to inhabit visions and project endings, but we also need to remain aware of their provisionality and constructedness. Shakespeare explores this tension in all his late plays, but especially in *The Tempest*.

In *The Tempest*, Prospero, who rules over an island of magic creatures after having been exiled from Milan by his usurping brother, has spent the play believing himself capable of directing a full cast of characters (including his shipwrecked brother and the royal household of Naples) to an apocalyptic showdown and happy ending on the stage of his island. But at the theatrical climax of his production – an iconic, symbol-laden wedding masque for his daughter Miranda and the prince of Naples, Ferdinand – he discovers that he has been trapped in his own illusion of power. The island he has thought to be under his control is, he suddenly realizes, like a theatre not in the sense that both are sites of revelation and order, but in the sense that both lack substance and durability; both can be cleared like a stage at the end of a play. When Prospero discovers the plot on his life that has unfolded behind the scenes, he concedes that his plot was merely a daydream. He, his island, and his whole world

shall dissolve,
And like this insubstantial pageant faded,
Leave not a rack behind. We are such stuff
As dreams are made on, and our little life
Is rounded with a sleep.[31]

This moment of anagnorisis is overtaken by happy developments. In its final act, the play flowers into an ending of joy beyond hope, expressed with wonder by the ageing Gonzalo:

Was Milan thrust from Milan that his issue
Should become kings of Naples? O rejoice
Beyond a common joy, and set it down
With gold on lasting pillars! In one voyage
Did Claribel her husband find at Tunis,
Ferdinand, her brother, found a wife
Where he himself was lost, Prospero his dukedom
In a poor isle, and all of us ourselves
When no man was his own.[32]

Profound though this joy may be, Prospero's tragi-comic recognition has not yet run its course. The theatrical epilogue is usually a slight, marginal form, common in Elizabethan drama as an invitation to applause; however, in *The Tempest*, it becomes a stunning piece of meta-theatre. It is in the epilogue that Prospero comes face to face with the full significance of his earlier recognition. He acknowledges his infirmity anew, now not because of the wreck of a play he has directed, but because of the end of the play he has lived. Like Ariel, with whom he repeatedly identifies in this speech, Prospero, too, is a thing of the theatre and must vanish with the play. In the epilogue, he abandons the attempt to authenticate himself by staging a re-enactment of his history, and instead simply accepts his place in it. His remaining strength is 'most faint' not only because he is left unable to control others, but because, more painfully, he cannot even authenticate his own existence without a free extension of acknowledgement by the audience. And this acknowledgement is double-edged: the audience can affirm his worthiness to return to Milan only with a gesture which, at the same time, looks beyond him to the actor on stage: by clapping, they simultaneously validate and end Prospero's existence.

In this moment of recognition, it is not Prospero alone who is required to let go. His request also demands a surrender from the audience. By sanctioning the disso-lution of the play, we give up the only medium by which the *Tempest*'s characters are present to us and thus, like Prospero, surrender the (illusory) power to oversee the presence of others. This acceptance is caught up with a yet more intimate confession. By soliciting the audience's prayer for his soul, like one dying, Prospero associates the end of a performance with the hour of death. By doing so, he turns our acknowledgement of his theatricality into a premonition of our own transience, our own part in a world – yea this great Globe itself – which tends towards dissolution. This gently exposes the desire to control and perpetuate presence as springing from a deeper denial of mortality which can only be offered to the mercy of God.

This double movement overcomes the Cavellian tempta-tion of theatricalization. As discussed in Chapter 2, Cavell

THE END OF IMAGES

THE END OF IMAGES

reads the condition of the theatre – figures represented on a stage, observed by an audience – as a literalization of the human temptation to do precisely this with the people in one's life, not least those one loves: to act as if one could survey them wholly, from a position of safety, to direct their coming and going without exposure or risk to oneself. For Cavell, many of Shakespeare's tragic protagonists are in the grip of exactly this temptation: the 'theatricalization' of their loved ones. King Lear must have his daughters' love declaimed on stage; Othello and Leontes must direct and interpret their wives' actions with authority. None of them can bear the ambiguity, uncertainty, and elusiveness of their loved ones, the inability to summon, survey, and control them. For Cavell, Shakespeare's tragedies are a therapy for the audience, allowing them to recognize and be purged of their own tendencies to do this.

My own approach is slightly different. What we need is not so much to disavow theatricality (as if a mere authenticity were possible), but both to hold on and let go. It is precisely this double movement, enabled by a sophisticated meta-theatricality, which creates the distinctive magic of Shakespeare's late plays. This is nowhere more poignant than in *The Winter's Tale*, where Hermione's resurrection (as I argued in Chapter 2) is indissolubly both a real resurrection and a theatrical one. Paulina's words 'It is required you do awake your faith', addressed to both characters and audience, are an exhortation at once to quasi-religious faith and to a quasi-Coleridgean suspension of disbelief in a theatrical event.[33] The audience can only experience the reality of this resurrection by also and at the same time acknowledging its theatricality. Both are true. Here, as in all his late plays, Shakespeare counters the lure of a possessive imagination by giving his audiences imaginative *work*, offering them an experience of reconciliation, recognition, and resurrection, but only at the price of holding it lightly and not coming to rest in it.

The pain of letting go (like the sadness at the end of a great novel) is not irrelevant to this experience, but bracing. What is more, it can itself become a site of encounter that spans worlds. In the mature plays of Shakespeare, it is precisely the shared pain of experiencing the limits of art's power to make the world present which creates the most vulnerable space of encounter between author, performer, and audience. This space, hovering at the threshold between play world and ordinary world, is there and gone: it can't be held. But its memory can become an anticipation.

> Now I want
> Spirits to enforce, art to enchant,
> And my ending is despair,
> Unless I be relieved by prayer,
> Which pierces so that it assaults
> Mercy itself, and frees all faults.
> As you from crimes would pardoned be,
> Let your indulgence set me free.[34]

There is perhaps no encounter between character, actor, audience, and author in all the canon of Shakespeare that is more poignant.

Both *The Winter's Tale* and *The Tempest* validate a deeply held desire for (self-)revelation and communion, without pretending that this desire finds a resting place either in the theatre or in ordinary life. They hold a tension between finding and making: between witnessing to a promise extended from beyond human construction on the one hand, and creating a consciously theatrical image on the other. Their luminous other-worlds throw an eschatological light on the ordinary world, which appears, for a moment, as itself only an ephemeral image of a greater reality to come. 'When the author walks on to the stage', as C. S. Lewis says, 'the play is over.'[35] In this way, Shakespeare's self-dissolving images encourage their audience to sustain a dialectic of eschatological expectation: neither to pre-empt nor to despair of the realization of an eschatological consummation acknowledged as impossible within present conditions.

Notes

1. The Apostles' Creed, third article.
2. Aquinas, *Summa Theologiae* 2–1.114.2. There is a long and ongoing debate about the question of whether it is theologically admissible or necessary to posit a 'natural desire for the supernatural' or a natural vocation that can only be realized supernaturally. In the twentieth and twenty-first centuries, this debate has had its primary focal point in Henri de Lubac's *Surnaturel* and related writings. John Milbank gives a strong defence of the necessity of such an argument in *The Suspended Middle* (Grand Rapids, MI: Eerdmans, 2nd ed., 2014) and elsewhere. For an overview of the debate, see e.g. Nicholas J. Healy, 'The Christian Mystery of Nature and Grace,' in *T&T Clark Companion to Henri de Lubac*, edited by Jordan Hillebert (London: T&T Clark, 2021), ch. 7.

3. Lewis, *Mere Christianity*, II.5.
4. E.g. Isaiah 2; Micah 4; Matthew 7; Matthew 25; Luke 13; Revelation 20.
5. E.g. Jeremiah 29; Psalm 126; and many others.
6. E.g. Ezekiel 40; Revelation 21.
7. E.g. 1 Kings 4.25; Isaiah 36.16; Micah 4.4.
8. E.g. Daniel 7.
9. E.g. Revelation 6.
10. E.g. Revelation 20.
11. E.g. Romans 8, probably alluding to Isaiah 9.6; Colossians 1.
12. 1 Corinthians 15.
13. 1 Corinthians 13.14; Colossians 3.3–5; 1 John 3.2.
14. Revelation 22.17, 22.20.
15. For more detailed readings of the following three works, see my commentary on Revelation 20.11–15, 'The Spirit and the Bridge Say Come,' in Ben Quash (ed.), *Visual Commentary on Scripture* (London: The Visual Commentary on Scripture Foundation, 2018), https://thevcs.org/last-judgement/spirit-and-bride-say-come. On the reception of apocalyptic texts in art and literature, see also e.g. Christopher Rowland, 'Imagining the Apocalypse,' *New Testament Studies* 51, no. 3 (2005), 303–327; Christopher Rowland, 'Apocalyptic Literature,' in *The Oxford Handbook of English Literature and Theology*, edited by David Jasper, Elisabeth Jay, and Andrew Hass (Oxford: Oxford University Press, 2007), 342–360; Heidi J. Hornik, 'Eschatology in Fine Art,' in *The Oxford Handbook of Eschatology*, edited by Jerry Walls (Oxford: Oxford University Press, 2008), 629–654; Anthony O'Hear and Natasha O'Hear, *Picturing the Apocalypse: The Book of Revelation in the Arts over Two Millennia* (Oxford: Oxford University Press, 2015); Lorenzo DiTommaso, 'Apocalyptic Literature in the Global Imagination,' in *A Companion to*

World Literature, edited by Ken Seigneurie (Oxford: Wiley-Blackwell, 2020), 215–226.

16. Rainer Marie Rilke, 'Archäischer Torso Apollos,' in *Neue Gedichte* (Leipzig: Insel-Verlag, 1907), translated by Mitchell as 'Archaic Torso of Apollo' in *The Selected Poetry of Rainer Maria Rilke*, 60–61. On Michelangelo's Jesus as Apollo, see John W. Dixon, 'The Christology of Michelangelo: The Sistine Chapel,' *Journal of the American Academy of Religion* 55, no. 3 (1987), 503–533.

17. William Blake, 'A Vision of the Last Judgement,' in *Life of William Blake*, edited by Alexander Gilchrist (London: Macmillan, 1863), 2:193.

18. The question of hope – whether it is at heart a virtue or a form of self-delusion – has animated philosophy and theology since the myth of Pandora's Box in Hesiod's *Works and Days*. Significant twentieth-century literature includes Ernst Bloch, *Das Prinzip Hoffnung* (Frankfurt: Suhrkamp, 1954), translated by Neville Plaice, Stephen Plaice, and Paul Knight as *The Principle of Hope* (Oxford: Blackwell, 1986); Jürgen Moltmann, *Theologie der Hoffnung* (Munich: Christian Kaiser, 1964), translated by James W. Leitch as *Theology of Hope: On the Ground and the Implications of a Christian Eschatology* (London: SCM Press, 1967); Dora Panofsky and Erwin Panofsky, *Pandora's Box: The Changing Aspects of a Mythical Symbol* (Princeton, NJ: Princeton University Press, 1956); Gabriel Marcel, *Homo Viator: Introduction to the Metaphysic of Hope*, translated by Emma Craufurd (Chicago, IL: Henry Regnery, 1951); Jonathan Lear, *Radical Hope: Ethics in the Face of Cultural Devastation* (Cambridge, MA: Harvard University Press, 2006); Terry Eagleton, *Hope without Optimism* (New Haven, CT: Yale University Press, 2015). I have written about hope in twentieth-century

theology in Wolfe, 'Hope,' in *Edinburgh Critical History of Twentieth-Century Christian Theology*, edited by Philip Ziegler (Edinburgh: Edinburgh University Press, 2022), 333–344.

19. Tom Perrotta, *The Leftovers* (New York: St Martin's Press, 2011).
20. See e.g. Cormac McCarthy, *The Road* (New York: Alfred A. Knopf, 2006); Emily St John Mandel, *Station Eleven* (New York: Alfred A. Knopf, 2011).
21. On this quality of visual art, see Pfau, *Incomprehensible Certainty*.
22. This does not apply to forms of music that are deliberately cyclical or open-ended, whether in the non-Western traditions of Eastern and Southeast Asia, the Middle East, and Africa, or in some Western music, including certain forms of jazz, serialism, and minimalism. An ongoing debate surrounding the 'holy minimalism' of Henryk Górecki, Arvo Pärt, and John Tavener concerns the theological implications of such deliberate stasis or cyclicality. The critical case is presented in Jeremy S. Begbie, *Theology, Music and Time* (Cambridge: Cambridge University Press, 2000), 128–154; the positive case is presented e.g. in Paul Hillier, *Arvo Pärt: Out of Silence* (Oxford: Oxford University Press, 1997); Katherine Kennedy Steiner, 'Into His Great Silence,' *The Cresset* 77/3 (2014): 35–37; Peter Bouteneff, *Arvo Pärt: Out of Silence* (New York: St Vladimir's Seminary Press, 2015); Jūlija Jonāne, 'View on Sacred Minimalism and Music by Pēteris Vasks as Incarnation of Theological Ideas,' *Menotyra* 23, no. 3 (2016): 215–227. I am grateful to Sarah Moerman and Brian Robinette for some of these references.
23. Roger Scruton, *The Death-Devoted Heart: Sex and the Sacred in Wagner's Tristan and Isolde* (Oxford: Oxford University

Press, 2004), 99. For relevant analyses of the Ring cycle, see esp. Roger Scruton, *The Ring of Truth: The Wisdom of Wagner's Ring of the Nibelung* (London: Allen Lane, 2016); Philip Kitcher and Richard Schacht, *Finding an Ending: Reflections on Wagner's Ring* (Oxford: Oxford University Press, 2004).

24. See e.g. Bryan Magee, *Wagner and Philosophy* (London: Penguin, 2nd ed., 2001), 27; Scruton, *Ring of Truth*, ch. 4.

25. This partly underlies the repeated accusations of fraudulence levelled against Wagner by his famous detractors; see e.g. Friedrich Nietzsche, *Der Fall Wagner* (Leipzig: C. G. Naumann, 1895) and the literature it has engendered.

26. Too little has been written on this great subtitle of J. R. R. Tolkien's *The Hobbit, or There and Back Again* (London: Allen & Unwin, 1937). On Tolkien's meta-literary relation to the ordinary world and the world of faith, see Giuseppe Pezzini, *Tolkien and the Mystery of Literary Creation* (Cambridge: Cambridge University Press, 2024).

27. 1 John 3.2.

28. Colossians 3.3.

29. Originally published as Samuel Beckett, *En attendant Godot* (Paris: Les Éditions de Minuit, 1952), translated by the author as *Waiting for Godot* (London: Faber, corrected ed., 1965); Beckett, *Endgame* (London: Faber, 1958).

30. Shakespeare, *King Lear* 5.3.315–316.

31. William Shakespeare, *The Tempest*, edited by Stephen Orgel (Oxford: Oxford University Press, 1987), 4.1.146–158.

32. Shakespeare, *The Tempest* 5.1.205–213.

33. Shakespeare, *Winter's Tale* 5.3.94–95.

34. Shakespeare, *The Tempest*, epilogue. For a fuller reading of the eschatological meta-theatricality of *The Tempest*, see Judith Wolfe, "'Like This Insubstantial Pageant Faded":

Eschatology and Theatricality in *The Tempest*,' *Literature and Theology* 18, no. 4 (2004), 371–382. See also Cynthia Marshall, *Last Things and Last Plays: Shakespearean Eschatology* (Carbondale, IL: Southern Illinois University Press, 1991). For a keen meta-theatrical reading of Beckett's late plays, see Erik Tonning, *Samuel Beckett's Abstract Drama: Works for Stage and Screen 1962–1985* (Bern: Peter Lang, 2007).

35. Lewis, *Mere Christianity*, II.5.

6 | Conclusion

We only live, only suspire
Consumed by either fire or fire.

T. S. Eliot, 'Little Gidding'

Who by Fire?

Shakespeare's drama matters not only for those who attend the theatre. Even if we have never seen their plays, we have experienced in our own lives something of what Shakespeare and Beckett attempt to capture on stage, in experiences of profound joy or insight which have, despite all their luminosity, dissolved. In beholding the glory of a natural scene, in an experience of spiritual oneness, or in falling deeply in love, existence is charged with a beauty and meaning that we experience, if at all, only as arriving from beyond our resources of sense-making.[1] Such experiences seem to come as a promise that reality transcends the cycle of death and decay, of fragmentation and construction; they make us say 'there is eternity' and 'for this I was made'. Rainer Maria Rilke writes about lovers:

You touch each other with such bliss because the caress
  shelters,
because the spot does not fade which you tenderly
Cover; because you sense, beneath it,
Pure permanence. So you promise yourselves eternity, almost,
From the embrace.[2]

And yet such experiences do not last. Though their very
essence (it seemed) was eternity, the passage of time does
not leave them intact, sometimes not even as memories:
they fade, suffocate, burn up, or appear, in the light of later
events, to have been deceptive. Whether we try to hold on
to them by repeated emotional stimulation or by erecting
the structures necessary for a continued life with nature,
art, God, or a lover, something of that first quality of eternity is, ironically, lost.

Rilke himself confronted this experience with bitter
acuity:

And yet, when you have
Borne the terror of first looks, and desire at the window,
And the first walk together, *one* time, through the garden:
Lovers, is it still you? When you raise yourselves
Each to the other's mouth – drink on drink –
How strangely the drinker slips away from the act.[3]

Requited love, Rilke argues, is consumed and dissipates.
It may make us glimpse eternity, but it cannot sustain the
image. Rilke therefore insists that love is perfected in being
renounced or unrequited. We can sustain the eternity love
promises, he thinks, only through the creation of art that
is born of the pain and beauty of ephemerality: in writing

poetry that will last, we do what requited love cannot, namely to capture the revelatory intensity of experience in a way that witnesses to its momentariness, yet always renews itself.[4]

This counsel of renunciation is, in some sense, heroic. And yet for all Rilke's courage, it is ultimately also cowardly. To realize that the mirrors in which we see eternity are brittle must not mean either denying what we see in them or insisting that we can see without them. They are at once all we have and never adequate; and this leaves us always vulnerable. To secure ourselves by any means is futile. As C. S. Lewis, of all people, so bluntly put it:

> To love at all is to be vulnerable. Love anything, and your heart will certainly be wrung and possibly be broken. If you want to make sure of keeping it intact, you must give your heart to no one, not even to an animal. Wrap it carefully round with hobbies and little luxuries; avoid all entanglements; lock it up safe in the casket or coffin of your selfishness. But in that casket – safe, dark, motionless, airless – it will change. It will not be broken; it will become unbreakable, impenetrable, irredeemable. The alternative to tragedy, or at least to the risk of tragedy, is damnation.[5]

Finding, Making, Receiving

The world is poetic not only in the sense that God speaks it into being, but also in the sense that we are called to participate in its utterance. If experiences of glory or love are more than merely illusory, then they may suggest that our daily work of sense-making is, in part, a continual prolepsis to a wholeness that we have glimpsed but cannot recapture. And 'the sole wisdom for [one] who is haunted with ... the scent of unseen roses', as George MacDonald put it, 'is *work*'.[6]

The day-to-day work of living does not leave the visions that incited it unchanged: vocations become jobs, girlfriends become mothers and grandmothers (or strangers), art and scholarship become livelihoods. Life is cast into patterns and roles. Yet these can become spaces of exploration, discovery, and growth when inhabited with a certain virtuosity; and this means, among other things, with a love that continues to attend to the things that do not make sense as well as the things that do. Such virtuosity balances a recognition that we cannot avoid the responsibility of sense-making and life-building with an acknowledgement that they are never quite enough. We can never fully repose on or fully share a life we have created, because sense remains fragmented, and the ways in which we keep the world and people present to ourselves are also, in part, forms of detainment. This is why sometimes (as for the theatregoers at the end of Shakespeare's late plays), it is in the acknowledged pain of our inability to make reality fully present that we find the most intimate community.

But the response this demands is not apathy or detachment. The necessary intertwining of finding and making that animates human perception, understanding, and life requires that we not eliminate the risk that is inherent in our imaginative inhabitation of the world – and certainly not the risk inherent in faith – but learn to live with it. It demands that we not simply be lukewarm or ambivalent in our involvement, but that we simultaneously hold on and let go. In a theological light, such a double movement may be possible only if there can be hope in a divine gift that comes to us beyond all finding and making. Ultimately, this is an eschatological promise: 'Behold, I make all things new.'[7] 'When Christ who is your life is revealed, then you also will be revealed with him in glory.'[8] This promise is both remote and at hand: it echoes in every gift of love freely given.

These difficulties and promises are made luminously present in Karen Blixen's story *Babette's Feast*. The main characters of this story face the opposite temptation as Shakespeare's flawed protagonists: rather than clinging too tightly to the people they love, they renounce them too readily. The daughters of a non-conformist Danish pastor and the pillars of their small fishing community, Martine and Philippa dismiss the suitors who would, they fear, involve them too much in the world, its glories, and pleasures. Instead, they ground their sense of value and self in lives of renunciation and self-sacrifice.

But the character who has lost and sacrificed most is the French refugee Babette, who was once (though this remains her secret) a chef of international renown in her native Paris. Babette uses a suddenly gained fortune to lavish on the sisters and their community, in their old age, an extravagance they never sought or expected: a feast in honour of their late revered pastor-father. Among the guests at this feast is the suitor of Martine's youth, Lorens Loewenhielm, who has come to experience his own much more worldly life (latterly as a general) as empty gain, and is seeking spiritual succour. Yet the education of his palate in the high circles in which he has moved, at court and on a long-past journey to Paris, allow him to act as interpreter of what those gathered are eating and drinking: to enable the Puritans to appreciate the quality of what they, in turn, enable him to receive not as a worldly but as a spiritual feast.

Filled with this feast, the old General Loewenhielm rises to invoke Psalm 85 in a vision of plenitude which, though received as a free gift of insight, could be received only after a long life of failure, separation, and hard work:

> Mercy and truth have met together. Righteousness and bliss shall kiss one another. Man, in his weakness and short-sightedness believes he must make choices in this life. He trembles at the risks he takes. We know that fear. But no. Our choice is of no importance. There comes a time when our eyes are opened and we come to realize that mercy is infinite. We need only await it with confidence and receive it with gratitude. Mercy imposes no conditions. And lo! Everything we have chosen has been granted to us. And everything we renounced has also been granted. Yes, we even receive back what we rejected. For mercy and truth have met together, and righteousness and bliss shall kiss one another.

This is a hope, a vision, a prophecy, whose power is felt with the full force of the journey of loss the characters have undergone in *Babette's Feast*. And yet that journey must be repeated in life, and without guarantees or knowledge of what the end will look like. Shakespeare, Rilke, Eliot, and Blixen cannot conjure eschatological fulfilment, but only assume and enable postures of openness, kindling in their audiences the courage to risk hope. And such hope, it seems to me, is indispensable for ordinary life well lived.

If we are committed to living in this world and loving it, we can only do so in hope that all is true, and nothing is yet fully itself. 'Courage, dear heart. There is nothing to be afraid of', as Aslan says to Lucy.⁹ Or, as the Chasidic song has it, 'The whole world is a very narrow bridge. And the main thing is not to be afraid.'¹⁰

Notes

1. This is what Jean-Luc Marion describes as 'saturated phenomena' or, more recently, as 'events'; see e.g. Marion, *Étant donné: Essai d'une phénoménologie de la donation* (Paris: Presses Universitaires de France, 1997); translated by Jeffrey L. Kosky as *Being Given: Toward a Phenomenology of Givenness* (Stanford, CA: Stanford University Press, 2002); Marion, *D'Ailleurs, la Révélation* (Paris: Grasset, 2020).
2. Rilke, 'Second Elegy,' ll. 60–65 (translation mine).
3. Rilke, 'Second Elegy,' ll. 65–70 (translation mine).
4. Rilke discusses this especially movingly in relation to the sculptures of Auguste Rodin; see 'Auguste Rodin,' in *Rainer Maria Rilke: Sämtliche Werke*, edited by Ernst Zinn (Berlin: Suhrkamp, 1965), 5:139–201.
5. Lewis, *The Four Loves*, ch. 6.
6. George MacDonald, *Alec Forbes of Howglen* (London: Hurst & Blackett, 1865), 1:33.
7. Revelation 21.5 (KJV).
8. Colossians 3.4.
9. Lewis, *The Voyage of the Dawn Treader*, ch. 12.
10. Baruch Chait, 'Kol haOlam Kulo,' based on a saying by Rabbi Nachman of Breslov recorded in *Likutei Moharan* II, 48:2.

Reepicheep answered: "My own plans are made. While I can, I sail east in the Dawn Treader. When she fails me, I paddle east in my coracle. When she sinks, I shall swim east with my four paws. And when I can swim no longer, if I have not reached Aslan's country, or shot over the edge of the world in some vast cataract, I shall sink with my nose to the sunrise."

Bibliography

Alloa, Emmanuel. *Das durchscheinende Bild: Konturen einer Medialen Phänomenologie*. Zurich: Diaphanes Verlag, 2018.

Aquinas, Thomas. *Summa Theologiae: Latin Text and English Translation, Introductions, Notes, Appendices, and Glossaries*. Edited and translated by Thomas Gilby et al. 61 vols. London: Blackfriars with Eyre & Spottiswoode, 1964–1981.

Aquino, Fred, and Gabriel Gavrilyuk, eds. *Perceiving Things Divine: Towards a Constructive Account of Spiritual Perception*. Oxford: Oxford University Press, 2022.

Arendt, Hannah. *Eichmann in Jerusalem, Or: The Banality of Evil*. New York: Viking, 1963.

Augustine. *Confessions*. Translated by Henry Chadwick. Oxford: Oxford University Press, 2008.

Azevedo, Ruben T., and Manos Tsakiris. 'Art Reception as an Interoceptive Embodied Predictive Experience.' *Behavioral and Brain Sciences* 40, no. e350 (2017). https://doi.org/10.1017/s0140525x17001856.

Badura, Christopher, and Amy Kind, eds. *Epistemic Uses of Imagination*. London: Routledge, 2021.

Bancalari, Stefano, ed. 'Religion et "Attitude Naturelle".' *Archivio di Filosofia* 90, nos. 2–3 (2022).

Banham, Gary. *Kant's Transcendental Imagination*. London: Palgrave Macmillan, 2005.

Barfield, Owen, and Clive Staples Lewis. *The 'Great War' of Owen Barfield and C.S. Lewis: Philosophical Writings, 1927–1930.* Edited by Norbert Feinendegen and Arend Smilde. *Inklings Studies Supplements* 1 (2019).

Barth, J. Robert. *The Symbolic Imagination and the Romantic Tradition.* Princeton, NJ: Princeton University Press, 1977.

Bauman, Zygmunt. *Liquid Modernity.* Cambridge: Polity, 2000.

Beauvoir, Simone. *La deuxième sex.* 2 vols. Paris: Gallimard, 1949. *The Second Sex.* Translated by H. M. Parshley. London: Cape, 1953.

Beckett, Samuel. *En attendant Godot.* Paris: Les Éditions De Minuit, 1952.

Endgame. London: Faber, 1958.

Play. London: Faber, 1963.

Waiting for Godot. Translated by Samuel Beckett. Corrected ed. London: Faber, 1965.

Begbie, Jeremy S. *Theology, Music and Time.* Cambridge: Cambridge University Press, 2000.

Belting, Hans. *Face and Mask: A Double History.* Translated by Thomas S. Hansen and Abby J. Hansen. Princeton, NJ: Princeton University Press, 2017.

Blake, William. 'A Vision of the Last Judgement.' In *Life of William Blake,* edited by Alexander Gilchrist, 185–202. 2 vols. London: Macmillan, 1863.

Blanchette, Oliva. *Maurice Blondel: A Philosophical Life.* Grand Rapids, MI: William B. Eerdmans, 2010.

Bloch, Ernst. *Das Prinzip Hoffnung.* Frankfurt: Suhrkamp, 1954. *The Principle of Hope.* Translated by Neville Plaice, Stephen Plaice, and Paul Knight. Oxford: Blackwell, 1986.

Blondel, Maurice. *Action: Essay on a Critique of Life and a Science of Practice.* Translated by Oliva Blanchette. South Bend, IN: Notre Dame University, 1984.

L'Action: Essai d'une critique de la vie et d'une science de la pratique. Paris: F. Alcan, 1893.

Bonhoeffer, Dietrich. *Letters and Papers from Prison.* Translated by Isabel Best. Minneapolis, MI: Fortress, 2010.

Widerstand und Ergebung: Briefe und Aufzeichnungen aus der Haft. 2nd ed. Munich: Christian Kaiser, 1970.

Bouteneff, Peter. *Arvo Pärt: Out of Silence.* New York: St Vladimir's Seminary Press, 2015.

Bowker, John. *The Religious Imagination and the Sense of God.* Oxford: Oxford University Press, 1978.

Broughton, Janet. 'Impressions and Ideas.' In *The Blackwell Guide to Hume's Treatise,* edited by Saul Traiger. Oxford: Blackwell, 2006.

Burns, Timothy, Thomas Szanto, Alessandro Salice, Maxime Doyon, and Augustin Dumont, eds. *The Imagination: Kant's Phenomenological Legacy.* Vol. 17, pt. 2 of *The New Yearbook for Phenomenology and Phenomenological Philosophy.* London: Routledge, 2019.

Butler, Judith. *Bodies That Matter: On the Discursive Limits of 'Sex.'* London: Routledge, 1993.

Gender Trouble: Feminism and the Subversion of Identity. New York: Routledge, 1990.

Cannon, Jonathan, Amanda M. O'Brien, Lindsay Bungert, and Pawan Sinha. 'Prediction in Autism Spectrum Disorder: A Systematic Review of Empirical Evidence.' *Autism Research* 14, no. 4 (2021): 604–630.

Casey, Edward S. *Imagining: A Phenomenological Study.* Bloomington: Indiana University Press, 1976.

Catholic Church. *Catechism of the Catholic Church.* London: Catholic Truth Society, 1994.

Cavell, Stanley. *Cities of Words: Pedagogical Letters on a Register of the Moral Life.* Cambridge, MA: Harvard University Press, 2004.

Conditions Handsome and Unhandsome: The Constitution of Emersonian Perfectionism. Chicago, IL: University of Chicago Press, 1990.

Disowning Knowledge. Cambridge: Cambridge University Press, 2012.

In Quest of the Ordinary: Lines of Skepticism and Romanticism. Chicago, IL: University of Chicago Press, 1988.

Must We Mean What We Say? Cambridge: Cambridge University Press, 1969.

The Claim of Reason: Wittgenstein, Skepticism, Morality, and Tragedy. Oxford: Oxford University Press, 1979.

Celan, Paul. *Sprachgitter.* Frankfurt: S. Fischer Verlag, 1959.

Chabris, Christopher, and Daniel Simons. 'The Invisible Gorilla.' www.theinvisiblegorilla.com (accessed 17 January 2024).

Chalamet, Christophe, Andreas Dettwiler, Mariel Mazzocco, and Ghislain Waterlot, eds. *Game Over?: Reconsidering Eschatology.* Berlin: Walter de Gruyter, 2017.

Chalmers, David J. 'Perception and the Fall from Eden.' In *Perceptual Experience,* edited by Gendler Tamar Szabo, and John Hawthorne, 49–125. Oxford: Oxford University Press, 2006.

Clark, Andy. *Surfing Uncertainty: Prediction, Action, and the Embodied Mind.* Oxford: Oxford University Press, 2016.

Coakley, Sarah. *Sensing God? Reconsidering the Patristic Doctrine of 'Spiritual Sensation' for Contemporary Theology and Ethics.* The Père Marquette Lecture 2022. Milwaukee, WI: Marquette University Press, 2022.

Cohen, Elizabeth. 'Untitled.' Correspondence, private collection.

Cohen, Ted. *Thinking of Others: On the Talent for Metaphor.* Princeton, NJ: Princeton University Press, 2012.

Coleridge, Samuel T. *Biographia Literaria: Or, Biographical Sketches of My Literary Life and Opinions.* Edited by James

Engel, and W. Jackson Bate. 2 vols. Princeton, NJ: Princeton University Press, 1983.

Collini, Stefan. 'Beauty and the Footnote, Lecture 1: Justifications.' University of St Andrews, 11 October 2022.

Collins, John J. *The Apocalyptic Imagination: An Introduction to Jewish Apocalyptic Literature.* Grand Rapids, MI: William B. Eerdmans, 2016.

Costelloe, Timothy M. *The Imagination in Hume's Philosophy.* Edinburgh: Edinburgh University Press, 2018.

Cottingham, John. *In Search of a Soul: A Philosophical Essay.* Princeton, NJ: Princeton University Press, 2020.

Crowther, Paul. *The Phenomenology of Modern Art: Exploding Deleuze, Illuminating Style.* London: Continuum, 2012.

Currie, Gregory. *Imagining and Knowing: The Shape of Fiction.* Oxford: Oxford University Press, 2020.

Darwin, Charles. *The Origin of the Species.* London: John Murray, 1859.

Dawkins, Richard. *The Selfish Gene.* 4th ed. Oxford: Oxford University Press, 2016.

Deacy, Christopher. *Screening the Afterlife: Theology, Eschatology, and Film.* London: Routledge, 2012.

Deleuze, Gilles, and Félix Guattari. *Capitalisme et Schizophrénie: L'Anti-Œdipe.* Paris: Les Éditions De Minuit, 1972.

De Lubac, Henri. *Surnaturel: Études historiques.* Paris: Aubier, 1946.

Anti-Oedipus. Translated by Robert Hurley, Mark Seem, and Helen R. Lane. Minneapolis, MN: University of Minnesota Press, 1972.

Dennett, Daniel. *Darwin's Dangerous Idea: Evolution and the Meanings of Life.* London: Simon & Schuster, 1995.

Dima, Danai, Jonathan P. Roiser, Detlef E. Dietrich, Catharina Bonnemann, Heinrich Lanfermann, Hinderk M. Emrich, and Wolfgang Dillo. 'Understanding Why Patients with Schizophrenia Do Not Perceive the Hollow-Mask Illusion Using Dynamic Causal Modelling.' *NeuroImage* 46, no. 4 (March 2009): 1180–1186. https://doi.org/10.1016/j .neuroimage.2009.03.033.

Dion, Kenneth L., and Karen K. Dion. 'The Honi Phenomenon Revisited: Factors Underlying the Resistance to Perceptual Distortion of One's Partner.' *Journal of Personality and Social Psychology* 33, no. 2 (1976): 170–177. https://doi .org/10.1037/0022-3514.33.2.170.

DiTommaso, Lorenzo. 'Apocalyptic Literature in the Global Imagination.' In *A Companion to World Literature*, edited by Ken Seigneurie, 215–226. Oxford: Wiley-Blackwell, 2020.

Dixon, John W. 'The Christology of Michelangelo: The Sistine Chapel.' *Journal of the American Academy of Religion* 55, no. 3 (1987): 503–533. https://doi.org/10.1093/jaarel/lv.3.503.

Donoghue, Denis. *Metaphor*. Cambridge, MA: Harvard University Press, 2014.

Eagleton, Terry. *Hope without Optimism*. New Haven, CT: Yale University Press, 2016.

eChalk. 'The Rotating Mask Illusion.' YouTube, 20 July 2012. www.youtube.com/watch?v=sKaoeaKsdAo (accessed 17 January 2024).

Eliot, George. *Middlemarch*. Edinburgh: William Blackwood, 1872.

Eliot, Thomas Stearns. *Four Quartets*. London: Faber, 1941.

'Religion and Literature.' In *Faith That Illuminates*, edited by Vigo A. Demant, 29–54. London: Centenary, 1935.

'Religion and Literature.' In *The Complete Prose of T.S. Eliot, Volume 5: Tradition and Orthodoxy, 1943–1939*, edited by Iman Javadi, Ronald Schuchard, and Jayme Stayer, 218–229. Baltimore, MD: Johns Hopkins University Press, 2017.

Ellis, Willis Davis, ed. *A Source Book of Gestalt Psychology.* London: Kegan Paul, Trench, Trubner & Co., 1938.

Falconer, Morgan. *Why Your Five Year Old Could Not Have Done That: Modern Art Explained.* London: Thames & Hudson, 2012.

Farrer, Austin. *The Glass of Vision.* Glasgow: Glasgow University Press, 1948.

Fauconnier, Gilles and Mark Turner. *The Way We Think: Conceptual Blending and the Mind's Hidden Complexities.* New York: Basic Books, 2002.

Felstiner, John. *Paul Celan: Poet, Survivor, Jew.* New Haven, CT: Yale University Press, 2001.

Ferreyrolles, Gérard. *Les reines du monde: L'imagination et la coutume chez Pascal.* Paris: Honoré Champion, 1995.

Fiddes, Paul S. *The Promised End: Eschatology in Theology and Literature.* Oxford: Blackwell, 2000.

Foucault, Michel. *L'archéologie du savoir.* Paris: Gallimard, 1969.

The Archaeology of Knowledge & the Discourse on Language. Translated by A. M. Sheridan Smith. New York: Pantheon Books, 1972.

Les mots et les choses: Une archéologie des sciences humaines. Paris: Gallimard, 1966.

The Order of Things: An Archaeology of the Human Sciences. New York: Pantheon, 1970.

Frigo, Alberto. 'Necessary Error: Pascal on Imagination and Descartes's Fourth Meditation.' *Early Modern French Studies* 39, no. 1 (July 2017): 31–44. https://doi.org/10.1080/2 0563035.2017.1318474.

Gadamer, Hans-Georg. *Truth and Method.* Translated by Joel C. Weinsheimer and Donald G. Marshall. London: Continuum, 2004.

Gendler, Tamar Szabó. *Intuition, Imagination, and Philosophical Methodology.* Oxford: Oxford University Press, 2010.

Gendler, Tamar Szabó, and John Hawthorne, eds. *Perceptual Experience.* Oxford: Oxford University Press, 2006.

Gerhart, Mary, and Allan Melvin Russell. *Metaphoric Process: The Creation of Scientific and Religious Understanding.* Fort Worth, TX: Texas Christian University Press, 1984.

Gibson, James J. *The Senses Considered as Perceptual Systems.* London: Allen & Unwin, 1966.

Gilchrist, Alexander, ed. *Life of William Blake.* 2 vols. London: Macmillan, 1863.

Golomb, Jacob. *In Search of Authenticity: From Kierkegaard to Camus.* London: Routledge, 1995.

In Search of Authenticity: From Kierkegaard to Camus. London: Routledge, 2016.

Gombrich, Ernst H. *Art and Illusion: A Study in Psychology of Pictorial Representation.* 2nd ed. London: Phaedon, 1961.

Goodman, Nelson. *Languages of Art.* Indianapolis, IN: Hackett Publishing Company, 1976.

Gregor-Dellin, Martin, and Dietrich Mack, eds. *Cosima Wagner's Diaries.* London: Harcourt Brace Jovanovich, 1978.

Guignon, Charles B. *On Being Authentic.* London: Routledge, 2004.

Harari, Yuval N. *Homo Deus: A Brief History of Tomorrow.* London: Vintage Books, 2016.

Sapiens: A Brief History of Mankind. London: Vintage, 2014.

Hart, Trevor A., Jeremy Begbie, and Gavin Hopps, eds. *Art, Imagination and Christian Hope: Patterns of Promise.* Aldershot: Ashgate, 2012.

Hawley, Katherine. *How to Be Trustworthy.* Oxford: Oxford University Press, 2020.

Heaney, Seamus. *Death of a Naturalist.* London: Faber, 1966.

Hedley, Douglas. *The Iconic Imagination*. London: Bloomsbury Academic, 2016.

Heidegger, Martin. *Sein Und Zeit*. Halle: Niemeyer, 1927. *Being and Time*. Translated by John Macquarrie and Edward Robinson. Oxford: Blackwell, 1962.

Hick, John. 'Religious Faith as Experiencing-As.' *Royal Institute of Philosophy Lectures* 2 (1968): 20–35. https://doi.org/10.1017/s0080443600010864.

Hillebert, Jordan, ed. *T&T Clark Companion to Henri de Lubac*. London: T&T Clark, 2021.

Hillier, Paul. *Arvo Pärt*. Oxford: Oxford University Press, 1997.

Hohwy, Jakob. 'The Predictive Processing Hypothesis.' In *The Oxford Handbook of 4E Cognition*, edited by Albert Newen, Leon De Bruin, and Shaun Gallagher, 129–146. Oxford: Oxford University Press, 2018.

Holyoak, Keith. *The Spider's Thread: Metaphor in Mind, Brain, and Poetry*. Boston, MA: MIT Press, 2019.

Homann, Karl. 'Zum Begriff Einbildungskraft nach Kant.' *Archiv für Begriffsgeschichte* 14 (1970): 266–302. www.jstor.org/stable/24358342.

Hornik, Heidi J. 'Eschatology in Fine Art.' In *The Oxford Handbook of Eschatology*, edited by Jerry L. Walls, 629–654. Oxford: Oxford University Press, 2008.

Horstmann, Rolf-Peter. *Kant's Power of Imagination*. Cambridge: Cambridge University Press, 2018.

Hume, David. *A Treatise of Human Nature*. Edited by David Fate Norton and Mary J. Norton. Oxford: Clarendon, 2007.

Husserl, Edmund. *Die Krisis der europäischen Wissenschaften und die transzendentale Phänomenologie Eine Einleitung in die phänomenologische Philosophie*. The Hague: Martinus Nijhoff, 1954.

The Crisis of European Sciences and Transcendental Phenomenology: An Introduction to Phenomenological Philosophy. Translated by David Carr. Evanston, IL: Northwestern University Press, 1970.

Insole, Chris. *Negative Natural Theology.* Oxford: Oxford University Press, 2025.

Iosifyan, Marina, Anton Sidoroff-Dorso, and Judith Wolfe. 'Cross-Modal Associations between Paintings and Sounds: Effects of Embodiment.' *Perception* 42, no. 1 (October 2022): 030100662211264. https://doi.org/10.1177/03010066221126452.

Iosifyan, Marina, and Judith E. Wolfe. 'Buffering Effect of Fiction on Negative Emotions: Engagement with Negatively Valenced Fiction Decreases the Intensity of Negative Emotions.' *Cognition and Emotion* (2024): 1–18. https://doi.org/10.1080/02699931.2024.2314986.

'Everyday Life vs Art: Effects of Perceptual Context on the Mode of Object Interpretation.' *Empirical Studies of the Arts* 42, no. 1 (2023): 166–191. https://doi.org/10.1177/0276237423117.

'Poetry vs Everyday Life: Context Increases Perceived Meaningfulness of Sentences,' under review.

Irenaeus. *Against the Heresies.* Translated by Alexander Roberts and W. H. Rambaut. Edinburgh: T&T Clark, 1868.

Ittelson, William H. *The Ames Demonstrations in Perception.* London: Hafner, 1952.

Janicaud, Dominique, ed. *Le Tournant théologique de la phénoménologie française.* Combas: Éditions de l'Éclat, 1991.

Phenomenology and the 'Theological Turn.' New York: Fordham University Press, 1991.

Jonāne, Jūlija. 'View on Sacred Minimalism and Music by Pēteris Vasks as Incarnation of Theological Ideas.' *Menotyra* 23, no. 3 (2016): 215–227.

Jones, David. *Epoch and Artist.* London: Faber, 1959.

Julian of Norwich. *Revelations of Divine Love.* Edited by Barry A. Windeatt. Oxford: Oxford University Press, 2015.

Kant, Immanuel. *Critique of Pure Reason.* Edited and translated by Paul Guyer and Allen W. Wood. Cambridge University Press: Cambridge, 1999.

Kritik der reinen Vernunft. Edition A 1781. Edition B, Riga: Harknoch, 1787.

Kermode, Frank. *The Sense of an Ending: Studies in the Theory of Fiction.* Oxford: Oxford University Press, 1967.

Kierkegaard, Søren. *Attack upon 'Christendom.'* Edited and translated by Walter Lowrie. Princeton, NJ: Princeton University Press, 1944.

Begrebet Angest: En simpel psychologisk-paapegende Overveielse i Retning af det dogmatiske. Copenhagen: C.A. Reitzel, 1843.

Philosophical Fragments, or, a Fragment of Philosophy. Translated by David Swenson and Howard Hong. Princeton, NJ: Princeton University Press, 1962.

Philosophiske Smuler. Copenhagen: C.A. Reitzel, 1844.

Sygdommen til Døden: En christelig psychologisk Udirkling til Opbyggelse og Opvækkelse. Copenhagen: C.A. Reitzel, 1849.

The Concept of Anxiety. Translated by Reidar Thomte. Princeton, NJ: Princeton University Press, 1980.

The Sickness unto Death. Translated by Edna H. Hong and Howard V. Hong. Princeton, NJ: Princeton University Press, 1983.

Kind, Amy. *Imagination and Creative Thinking.* Cambridge: Cambridge University Press, 2022.

ed. *The Routledge Handbook of Philosophy of Imagination.* London: Routledge, 2016.

Kind, Amy, and Peter Kung, eds. *Knowledge through Imagination.* Oxford: Oxford University Press, 2016.

Kitcher, Philip, and Richard Schacht. *Finding an Ending: Reflections on Wagner's Ring*. Oxford: Oxford University Press, 2004.

Kneller, Jane. *Kant and the Power of Imagination*. Cambridge: Cambridge University Press, 2007.

Koelsch, Stefan, Peter Vuust, and Karl Friston. 'Predictive Processes and the Peculiar Case of Music.' *Trends in Cognitive Sciences* 23, no. 1 (January 2019): 63–77. https://doi.org/10.1016/j.tics.2018.10.006.

Kripke, Saul A. *Wittgenstein on Rules and Private Language*. Oxford: Blackwell, 1982.

Kundera, Milan. *The Unbearable Lightness of Being*. Translated by Michael Henry Heim. New York: HarperCollins, 1984.

Laird, Martin. *Into the Silent Land*. London: Darton, Longman & Todd, 2006.

Lakoff, George, and Mark Johnson. *Metaphors We Live By*. Chicago, IL: University of Chicago Press, 1980.

Langland-Hassan, Peter. *Explaining Imagination*. Oxford: Oxford University Press, 2020.

Lear, Jonathan. *Radical Hope: Ethics in the Face of Cultural Devastation*. Cambridge, MA: Harvard University Press, 2006.

Leppänen, Jukka M., Maarten Milders, J. Stephen Bell, Emma Terriere, and Jari K. Hietanen. 'Depression Biases the Recognition of Emotionally Neutral Faces.' *Psychiatry Research* 128, no. 2 (2004): 123–133. https://doi.org/10.1016/j.psychres.2004.05.020

Levens, Sara M., and Ian H. Gotlib. 'Updating Positive and Negative Stimuli in Working Memory in Depression.' *Journal of Experimental Psychology: General* 139, no. 4 (2010): 654–664. https://doi.org/10.1037/a0020283.

Levinas, Emmanuel. *Totalité et infini: essai sur l'extériorité*. The Hague: Martinus Nijhoff, 1961.

Totality and Infinity: An Essay on Exteriority. Translated by Alphonso Lingis. Pittsburgh, PA: Duquesne University Press, 1969.

Lewis, Clive Staples. (as Clive Hamilton). *Spirits in Bondage: A Cycle of Lyrics.* London: Heinemann, 1919.

Lewis, Clive Staples. *The Pilgrim's Regress.* London: Geoffrey Bles, 3rd ed., 1943.

'Bluspels and Flalansferes: A Semantic Nightmare.' In *Rehabilitations and Other Essays,* 133–158. London: Geoffrey Bles, 1939.

Mere Christianity. London: Geoffrey Bles, 1952.

'Myth Became Fact.' In *God in the Dock,* 54–60. London: Fontana, 1979.

The Abolition of Man. Oxford: Oxford University Press, 1943.

The Four Loves. London: Geoffrey Bles, 1960.

The Literary Impact of the Authorised Version. London: Athlone Press, 1950.

The Voyage of the Dawn Treader. London: Geoffrey Bles, 1952.

Till We Have Faces. London: Geoffrey Bles, 1956.

'Transposition.' In *They Asked for a Paper: Papers and Addresses,* 166–182. London: Geoffrey Bles, 1962.

Lewis, Clive Staples, and Charles Williams. *Arthurian Torso.* Oxford: Oxford University Press, 1948.

Ludz, Ursula, ed. *Hannah Arendt / Martin Heidegger: Briefe 1925–1975.* 2nd ed. Frankfurt: Klostermann, 1999.

Luhrmann, Tanya M. *How God Becomes Real: Kindling the Presence of Invisible Others.* Princeton, NJ: Princeton University Press, 2020.

Luther, Martin. 'A Beautiful Sermon on the Reception of the Holy Sacrament.' In *Luther's Works,* edited by Jaroslav Pelikan and Helmut T. Lehmann, 37: 100–101. St. Louis, MO: Concordia Publishing House, 1955.

Lyotard, Jean-François. *La Condition postmoderne: Rapport sur le savoir*. Paris: Éditions de Minuit, 1979.

The Postmodern Condition: A Report on Knowledge. Trans. Geoffrey Bennington and Brian Massumi. Minneapolis, MN: University of Minnesota Press, 1984.

MacDonald, George. *Alec Forbes of Howglen*. 3 vols. London: Hurst & Blackett, 1865.

Magee, Bryan. *Wagner and Philosophy*. 2nd ed. London: Penguin, 2001.

Magri, Tito. *Hume's Imagination*. Oxford: Oxford University Press, 2022.

Maguire, Matthew William. *The Conversion of Imagination: From Pascal through Rousseau to Tocqueville*. Cambridge, MA: Harvard University Press, 2006.

Makkreel, Rudolf A. *Imagination and Interpretation in Kant: The Hermeneutical Import of the Critique of Judgment*. Chicago, IL: University Of Chicago Press, 1990.

Mandel, Emily St. John. *Station Eleven*. New York: Alfred A. Knopf, 2011.

Mann, Thomas. *Der Zauberberg*. Berlin: S. Fischer, 1924.

The Magic Mountain. Translated by T. H. Lowe-Porter. London: Secker & Warburg, 1928.

Marcel, Gabriel. *Homo Viator: Introduction to the Metaphysic of Hope*. Translated by Emma Craufurd. Chicago, IL: Henry Regnery, 1951.

Marion, Jean-Luc. *Étant donné: Essai d'une phénoménologie de la donation*. Paris: Presses Universitaires de France, 1997.

Being Given: Toward a Phenomenology of Givenness. Translated by Jeffrey L. Kosky. Stanford, CA: Stanford University Press, 2002.

D'Ailleurs, la Révélation. Paris: Grasset, 2020.

Maritain, Jacques. 'The Frontiers of Poetry.' In *Art and Scholasticism with Other Essays*, translated by James F. Scanlan, 68–94. London: Sheed & Ward, 1946.

Marshall, Cynthia. *Last Things and Last Plays: Shakespearean Eschatology*. Carbondale, IL: Southern Illinois University Press, 1991.

McCarthy, Cormac. *The Road*. New York: Alfred A. Knopf, 2006.

McInroy, Mark. *Balthasar on the Spiritual Senses: Perceiving Splendour*. Oxford: Oxford University Press, 2014.

Meagher, John. *Shakespeare's Shakespeare: How the Plays Were Made*. New York: Continuum, 1998.

Merleau-Ponty, Maurice. 'Eye and Mind.' In *The Merleau-Ponty Aesthetics Reader: Philosophy and Painting*, edited by Galen A. Johnson. Evanston, IL: Northwestern University Press, 1993.

Phénoménologie de la perception. Paris: Éditions Gallimard, 1945.

Phenomenology of Perception: An Introduction. Translated by Colin Smith. London: Routledge, 1962.

Milbank, John. *The Suspended Middle*. 2nd ed. Grand Rapids, MI: William. B. Eerdmans, 2014.

Miller, M. and A. Clark. 'Happily Entangled: Prediction, Emotion, and the Embodied Mind.' *Synthese* 195 (2018): 2559–2575. https://doi.org/10.1007/s11229-017-1399-7

Moltmann, Jürgen. *Theologie Der Hoffnung*. Munich: Christian Kaiser, 1964.

Theology of Hope: On the Ground and the Implications of a Christian Eschatology. Translated by James W. Leitch. London: SCM Press, 1967.

Moran, Richard. *The Philosophical Imagination: Selected Essays*. Oxford: Oxford University Press, 2017.

Mörchen, Hermann. *Die Einbildungskraft Bei Kant*. Berlin: Walter de Gruyter, 1970.

Mulhall, Stephen. *On Being in the World: Wittgenstein and Heidegger on Seeing Aspects*. London: Routledge, 1993.

The Routledge Guidebook to Heidegger's Being and Time. 2nd ed. London: Routledge, 2013.

Wittgenstein's Private Language: Grammar, Nonsense, and Imagination in Philosophical Investigations, Sections 243–315. Oxford: Oxford University Press, 2007.

Murdoch, Iris. *The Sovereignty of the Good*. London: Routledge, 1970.

Nichols, Shaun, ed. *The Architecture of the Imagination: New Essays on Pretence, Possibility, and Fiction*. Oxford: Oxford University Press, 2006.

Nietzsche, Friedrich. *Der Fall Wagner*. Leipzig: C. G. Naumann, 1895.

Nussbaum, Martha C. *Upheavals of Thought: The Intelligence of Emotions*. Cambridge: Cambridge University Press, 2001.

O'Hear, Natasha, and Anthony O'Hear. *Picturing the Apocalypse: The Book of Revelation in the Arts over Two Millennia*. Oxford: Oxford University Press, 2015.

Oliver, Simon. *Given Life: From Phenomenology to Theology*. Oxford: Oxford University Press, forthcoming.

Philosophy, God and Motion. London: Routledge, 2006.

Palamas, Gregory. 'On the Blessed Hesychasts.' In *Early Fathers from the Philokalia: Together with Some Writings of St. Abba Dorotheus, St. Isaac of Syria, and St. Gregory Palamas*. Translated by E. Kadloubovsky and G. E. H. Palmer. London: Faber, 1954.

Panofsky, Dora, and Erwin Panofsky. *Pandora's Box: The Changing Aspects of a Mythical Symbol*. Princeton, NJ: Princeton University Press, 1956.

Pascal, Blaise. *Pensées*. Edited by Philippe Sellier. Paris: Garnier, 1999.

Perrotta, Tom. *The Leftovers*. New York: St. Martin's Griffin, 2011.

Pezzini, Giuseppe. *Tolkien and the Mystery of Literary Creation*. Cambridge: Cambridge University Press, 2024.

Pfau, Thomas. *Incomprehensible Certainty: Metaphysics and Hermeneutics of the Image*. South Bend, IN: University of Notre Dame Press, 2022.

Pickstock, Catherine. *After Writing: On the Liturgical Consummation of Philosophy*. Oxford: Blackwell, 1998.

Pinkard, Terry. *Hegel's Phenomenology: The Sociality of Reason*. Cambridge: Cambridge University Press, 1994.

Pinkham, Amy E., Brensinger, Colleen, Kohler, Christian, Gur, Raquel E., and Gur, Ruben C. 'Actively Paranoid Patients with Schizophrenia Over-attribute Anger to Neutral Faces.' *Schizophrenia Research* 125, nos. 2–3 (2011): 174–178. https://doi.org/10.1016/j.schres.2010.11.006.

Plantinga, Alvin. *Warranted Christian Belief*. Oxford: Oxford University Press, 2000.

Plato. *The Republic*. Translated by Robin Waterfield. Oxford: Oxford University Press, 1994.

Polanyi, Michael. 'What Is a Painting?' *British Journal of Aesthetics* 10, no. 3 (1970): 225–236. https://doi.org/10.1093/bjaesthetics/10.3.225.

Pound, Ezra. 'In a Station of the Metro.' *Poetry: A Magazine of Verse* (1913).

Przywara, Erich. 'Drei Richtungen Der Phänomenologie.' *Stimmen Der Zeit* 115 (1928): 252–264.

Quine, Willard Van Orman. 'Two Dogmas of Empiricism.' *The Philosophical Review* 60 (1951): 20–43.

Richards, Ivor Armstrong. *Coleridge on Imagination*. London: Kegan Paul, Trench, Trubner & Co, 1934.

Ricœur, Paul. *Essays on Biblical Interpretation*. London: SPCK, 1981.

The Rule of Metaphor: The Creation of Meaning in Language. London: Routledge, 1986.

Rilke, Rainer Maria. 'Auguste Rodin.' In *Rainer Maria Rilke: Sämtliche Werke*, edited by Ernst Zinn, 5: 139–201, 6 vols. Berlin: Suhrkamp, 1965.

Briefe Aus Muzot, 1921 Bis 1926. Edited by Ruth Sieber-Rilke and Carl Sieber. Leipzig: Insel-Verlag, 1935.

Duineser Elegien. Leipzig: Insel-Verlag, 1923.

The Selected Poetry of Rainer Maria Rilke, translated by Stephen Mitchell. New York: Random House, 1980.

Robinette, Brian D. *Grammars of Resurrection: A Christian Theology of Presence and Absence*. New York: Crossroad / Herder & Herder, 2009.

The Difference Nothing Makes. South Bend, IN: University of Notre Dame Press, 2023.

Romanides, John. *Patristic Theology*. Thessaloniki: Uncut Mountain Press, 2008.

Rosa, Hartmut. *Unverfügbarkeit*. Berlin: Suhrkamp, 2018.

Rose, Gillian. *Love's Work*. New York: New York Review Books, 1995.

Rosen, Stanley. *The Elusiveness of the Ordinary: Studies in the Possibility of Philosophy*. New Haven, CT: Yale University Press, 2002.

Rowland, Christopher. 'Apocalyptic Literature.' In *The Oxford Handbook of English Literature and Theology*, edited by Andrew Hass, David Jasper, and Elisabeth Jay, 342–360. Oxford: Oxford University Press, 2007.

'Imagining the Apocalypse.' *New Testament Studies* 51, no. 3 (2005): 303–327. https://doi.org/10.1017/s0028688505000159.

Sartre, Jean-Paul. *L'Imagination*. Paris: Alcan, 1936.

L'Imaginaire: Psychologie phénoménologique de l'imagination. Paris: Gallimard, 1940.

Schjødt, Uffe. 'Predictive Coding in the Study of Religion.' *Supplements to Method & Theory in the Study of Religion* 7, no. 4 (2019): 364–379. https://doi.org/10.1163/9789004385375_025.

Schjødt, Uffe, and Marc Andersen. 'How Does Religious Experience Work in Predictive Minds?' *Religion, Brain & Behavior* 7, no. 4 (2017): 320–323. https://doi.org/10.1080/21 53599X.2016.1249913.

Schleiermacher, Friedrich. *Glaubenslehre.* 2nd ed. Gotha: Friedrich Andreas Perthes, 1831.

On Religion: Speeches to Its Cultured Despisers. Translated by Richard Crouter. Cambridge: Cambridge University Press, 1988.

The Christian Faith. Translated by H. R. Mackintosh and J. S. Stewart. Edinburgh: T&T Clark, 1928.

Reden über die Religion: An die Gebildeten unter ihren Verächtern. Gotha: Friedrich Andreas Perthes, 1799.

Scruton, Roger. *The Death-Devoted Heart: Sex and the Sacred in Wagner's Tristan and Isolde.* Oxford: Oxford University Press, 2004.

The Face of God: The Gifford Lectures 2010. London: Bloomsbury Continuum, 2014.

The Ring of Truth: The Wisdom of Wagner's Ring of the Nibelung. London: Allen Lane, 2016.

The Soul of the World. Princeton, NJ: Princeton University Press, 2016.

Shakespeare, William. *Pericles, Prince of Tyre.* Edited by Doreen DelVecchio and Antony Hammond. Cambridge: Cambridge University Press, 1998.

Shakespeare's Sonnets. Edited by Katherine Duncan-Jones. 2nd ed. London: Bloomsbury, 2010.

The Tempest. Edited by Stephen Orgel. Oxford: Oxford University Press, 1987.

The Tragedy of King Lear. Edited by Jay L. Halio. Cambridge: Cambridge University Press, 1992.

The Winter's Tale. Edited by Stephen Orgel. Oxford: Oxford University Press, 1996.

Simons, Daniel. *Selective Attention Test.* www.youtube.com/watch?v=vJG698U2Mvo (accessed 17 January 2024).

Sokolowski, Robert. *Introduction to Phenomenology.* Cambridge: Cambridge University Press, 1999.

Soskice, Janet. *Metaphor and Religious Language.* Oxford: Clarendon Press, 1985.

Stein, Edith. 'Husserls Phänomenologie und die Philosophie des Hl. Thomas von Aquino.' In *Festschrift, Edmund Husserl zum 70. Geburtstag gewidmet,* edited by Martin Heidegger. Halle: Niemeyer, 1929.

'Martin Heideggers Existenzphilosophie.' In *Endliches und Ewiges Sein: Versuch eines Aufstiegs zum Sinn des Seins,* edited by Andreas Uwe Müller. Freiburg: Herder, 2006.

Steiner, Katherine Kennedy. 'Into His Great Silence.' *The Cresset* 77, no. 3 (2014): 35–37.

Stock, Kathleen. *Only Imagine: Fiction, Interpretation and Imagination.* Oxford: Oxford University Press, 2017.

Streeter, Ryan. 'Heidegger's Formal Indication: A Question of Method in Being and Time.' *Man and World* 30 (1997): 413–430.

Tate, Andrew. *Apocalyptic Fiction.* London: Bloomsbury Academic, 2017.

Taylor, Charles. *A Secular Age.* Cambridge, MA: Harvard University Press, 2007.

Sources of the Self: The Making of the Modern Identity. Cambridge, MA: Harvard University Press, 1989.

The Ethics of Authenticity. Cambridge, MA: Harvard University Press, 1992.

The Language Animal. Cambridge, MA: Harvard University Press, 2016.

Thompson, Michael L., ed. *Imagination in Kant's Critical Philosophy.* Berlin: Walter de Gruyter, 2016.

Tolkien, John Ronald Reuel. *The Hobbit, or There and Back Again.* London: Allen & Unwin, 1937.

Tonning, Erik. *Samuel Beckett's Abstract Drama: Works for Stage and Screen 1962–1985.* Bern: Peter Lang, 2007.

Trilling, Lionel. *Sincerity and Authenticity.* London: Oxford University Press, 1972.

Van de Cruys, Sander, Claudia Damiano, Yannick Boddez, Magdalena Król, Lore Goetschalckx, and Johan Wagemans. 'Visual Affects: Linking Curiosity, Aha-Erlebnis, and Memory through Information Gain.' *Cognition* 212 (July 2021): 1046–1098. https://doi.org/10.1016/j.cognition.2021.104698.

Van de Cruys, Sander, and Johan Wagemans. 'Putting Reward in Art: A Tentative Prediction Error Account of Visual Art.' *I-Perception* 2, no. 9 (January 2011): 1035–1062. https://doi.org/10.1068/i0466aap.

Van Elk, Michael, and André Aleman. 'Brain Mechanisms in Religion and Spirituality: An Integrative Predictive Processing Framework.' *Neuroscience & Biobehavioral Reviews* 73 (February 2017): 359–378. https://doi.org/10.1016/j.neubiorev.2016.12.031.

Vonnegut, Kurt. *Mother Night.* New York: Avon, 1961.

Warnock, Mary. *Imagination.* London: Faber, 1976.

Weaver, Richard M. *Ideas Have Consequences.* Chicago, IL: University of Chicago Press, 1948.

Webster, John. *Confessing God: Essays in Christian Dogmatics II.* London: Bloomsbury T&T Clark, 2016.

God without Measure: God and the Works of God. 2 vols. London: Bloomsbury T&T Clark, 2016.

Williams, Rowan. *Being Human: Bodies, Minds, Persons.* Grand Rapids, MI: W. B. Eerdmans, 2018.

'Poetic and Religious Imagination.' *Theology* 80, no. 675 (May 1977): 178–187. https://doi.org/10.1177/0040571x7708000305.

The Edge of Words: God and the Habits of Language. London: Bloomsbury, 2014.

The Tragic Imagination. Oxford: Oxford University Press, 2016.

'Trinity and Revelation.' *Modern Theology* 2, no. 3 (1986): 197–212. https://doi.org/10.1111/j.1468-0025.1986.tb00114.x.

Wittgenstein, Ludwig. *Philosophical Investigations = Philosophische Untersuchungen.* Edited and translated by G. E. M. Anscombe. Oxford: Blackwell, 1953.

Wittreich, Warren J. 'The Honi Phenomenon: A Case of Selective Perceptual Distortion.' *Journal of Abnormal and Social Psychology* 47, no. 3 (July 1952): 705–712. https://doi.org/10.1037/h0058602.

Wolfe, Judith. *Heidegger and Theology.* London: T&T Clark, 2014.

'Hermione's Sophism: Ordinariness and Theatricality in *The Winter's Tale*.' *Philosophy and Literature* 39, no. 1A (2015): A83–105. https://doi.org/10.1353/phl.2015.0038.

'Hope.' In *The Edinburgh Critical History of Twentieth-Century Christian Theology*, edited by Philip G. Ziegler, 333–344. Edinburgh: Edinburgh University Press, 2022.

'Imagining God.' *Modern Theology* 40, no. 1 (2024). https://doi.org/10.1111/moth.12846.

'"Like This Insubstantial Pageant, Faded": Eschatology and Theatricality in *The Tempest*.' *Literature and Theology* 18, no. 4 (December 2004): 371–382. https://doi.org/10.1093/litthe/18.4.371.

'Pretense and Personhood: Theology and the Question of Authenticity.' Inaugural Lecture, University of St Andrews, 2022. www.youtube.com/watch?v=NmsoRusgaPM.

'The End of Images: Towards a Phenomenology of Eschatological Expectation.' In *Image as Theology: The Power of Art in Shaping Christian Thought, Devotion, and Imagination*, edited by Casey Strine, Mark McInroy, and Alexis Torrance. Turnhout: Brepols Publishers, 2022.

'The Eschatological Imagination in Literature.' *Religion and Literature*, forthcoming.

'"The Ordinary" in Stanley Cavell and Jacques Derrida.' *An Internet Journal of Philosophy* 17, no. 1 (2013): 250–268.

'The Renewal of Perception in Religious Faith and Biblical Narrative.' *European Journal for Philosophy of Religion* 13, no. 4 (December 2021). https://doi.org/10.24204/ejpr.2021.3744.

'The Spirit and the Bride Say Come.' In *The Visual Commentary on Scripture*, edited by Ben Quash, 111–128. London: The Visual Commentary on Scripture Foundation, 2018. https://thevcs.org/last-judgement/spirit-and-bride-say-come.

'Theology in *The Abolition of Man*.' In *Contemporary Perspectives on C. S. Lewis' The Abolition of Man*, edited by Gayne Anacker, and Tim Mosteller, 97–110. London: Bloomsbury, 2016.

Wunsch, Matthias. *Einbildungskraft und Erfahrung Bei Kant*. Berlin: Walter de Gruyter, 2012.

Zamir, Tzachi. *Acts: Theater, Philosophy, and the Performing Self*. Ann Arbor, MI: University of Michigan Press, 2014.

Double Vision: Moral Philosophy and Shakespearean Drama. Princeton, NJ: Princeton University Press, 2006.

Index

abstract art, 85–87
Alighieri, Dante, 135
ambiguity
  artistic. *See* imagination, art
  as essential to existence, 71–74
  linguistic, 71–74. *See also*
    metaphor
Ames Room, 13, 33, 79, 105
An Army Lines Up for Battle (Paul
  Noth), 17
An Old Woman with a Rosary
  (Paul Cezanne), 74
apocalyptic art, 132–141. *See also*
  eschatological art
  Autun Cathedral, 132
  Blake, William, 136–138
  Sistine Chapel, 141
  technological progress, 141
Apokalypse (Max Beckmann), 141
*Apokalypse II (Saint John's Vision
  of the Seven Candlesticks)*
  (Ernst Ludwig Kirchner), 140
Aquinas. *See* Thomas Aquinas,
  Saint
Aristotle, 112
art
  abstract, 85–87
  apocalyptic. *See*
    apocalyptic art

eschatological. *See* eschatological
  art
expressionism, 83
imaginative development,
  participation, 25, 74, 81–88,
  131, 145–146, 154
impressionism, 82–83
modern and postmodern art,
  85–87
At the Races (Édouard Manet), 83
authentic self. *See* selfhood,
  authentic self
authenticity, 23
  authentic self. *See* selfhood,
    authentic self
  as an ideal, 37–39
  ideal of authenticity, 64
  pretence, 67, 71
Autun Cathedral, 132

Babette's Feast (Karen Blixen),
  165–166
Balthasar, Hans Urs von, 111
Basho, Matsuo, 90
Beckett, Samuel, 149
  Endgame, 149
  Play, 56–59, 149
  Waiting for Godot, 149
Beckmann, Max, 141

Milbank, John, 155
modern art, 85–87
Mona Lisa (Leonardo da Vinci),
165–166
Morning, Interior (Maximillien
Luce), 74
mystical experience, 110, 115,
121

narrated self. *See* narrative roles
narrative roles, 38–42
limitations of, 39–40, 131
theological implications, 40–42,
61–62
narrative therapy, 39
Necker's cube, 78, 105
Nietzsche, Friedrich, 108
nous, 108

optical illusions, 78–80
Ames Room, 13, 33, 79, 105
duck–rabbit, 78, 105
Necker's cube, 78, 105
rotating mask, 79, 105
Origen, 110

perception
depth perception. *See* depth
perception
faces, 5–6, 29
images, 2–5, 76–78
ordinary, everyday, 2, 76–78
persons, 6–8, 106–107
sense, 2, 77–78
phenomenology, 34
Plantinga, Alvin, 118
poetry
depth perception, 91–92
imaginative development, 24,
91–93

postmodern art, 85–87
Pound, Ezra, 90
predictive processing, 31, 77–78, 99

Resurrection in Cookham (Sidney
Spencer), 141
Ricœur, Paul, 93, 96
Rilke, Rainer Maria, 91, 161
Duino Elegies, 1, 37, 67, 91, 105,
127, 161–163
role-playing, 24, 42–50
faith. *See* faith, Christian, role-
playing
narrative roles. *See* narrative
roles
social roles. *See* social roles
rotating mask, 79, 105

Schleiermacher, Friedrich, 108
Scripture
eschatological imagery, 130
imaginative development,
94–98
self-deception, 25
selfhood
authentic self, 23, 37–39, 50
buffered self, 40
eschatological dimensions,
148–149
narrated self. *See* narrative roles
role-playing. *See* role-playing
theatre in self-understanding.
See theatre, self-understanding
self-reflection, theatre. *See* theatre,
self-understanding
sense perception. *See* perception,
sense
sensus divinitatis, 108, 118
Seven Bowls of Wrath, The
(Heinrich Vogeler), 140